Soccer
THE MIND GAME

Advance praise for *Soccer – The Mind Game*

'This book will be a tremendous asset to both players and coaches who wish to know more about the psychology of football. It is well written and will be of immense benefit if performers follow up the reading with positive action.'
Andy Cale, FA Education Adviser

'*Soccer – The Mind Game* will provide an adrenalin-shot to a footballer's confidence, turning wannabes into world-beaters.'
Henry Winter, Football Correspondent, *The Daily Telegraph*

'This is a truly user-friendly book for the player and coach. Its "in a nutshell" simplicity provides football-specific information that people in the sport will understand and thrive on.'
Dean Riddle, Fitness Consultant, Leeds United

'A stunning book – packed with tips to motivate yourself and give yourself that ephemeral, essential "belief" which separates the great from the good. If you have aspirations – whether you play football or not – buy this book.'
Alison Kervin, Chief Sports Feature Writer, *The Times*

Soccer
THE MIND GAME

STEVE BULL • CHRIS SHAMBROOK

REEDSWAIN *Publishing*

This edition published in 2005 in the United States by
Reedswain Inc., 562 Ridge Road, Spring City, PA 19475

First published in 2004 by The Crowood Press Ltd,
Ramsbury, Marlborough, Wiltshire SN8 2HR

ISBN 1-59164-095-4

Library of Congress Control Number: 2005900333

Note
Whilst every effort has been made to ensure that this book is technically accurate and sound, neither the authors nor the publisher can accept responsibility for any injury or loss sustained as a result of using this material.

Typeset in Great Britain by Phoenix Typesetting, Auldgirth, Dumfriesshire

Printed and bound in Great Britain by Biddle's Ltd, King's Lynn

REEDSWAIN ***Publishing***
562 Ridge Road
Spring City, PA 19475 USA
1-800-331-5191
email: info@reedswain.com
www.reedswain.com

Contents

About the Authors

DR STEVE BULL

Steve Bull is an internationally recognized sport psychologist and a former member of the Football Association's Psychology Advisory Panel. He has served three times as Headquarters Psychologist for the Great Britain Olympic Team, his most recent appointment being for the 2004 Games in Athens. In the past twenty years, Steve has acted as consultant to a wide range of international sports teams including the England Cricket Team, the British Ski Team and the British Equestrian Team as well as individuals in Premiership Football and Rugby, the professional tennis circuit, the European PGA Golf Tour and professional motor sport. Steve also applies his work in the business world where he has consulted with more than ten different major organizations, providing executive coaching for senior management. He is regularly consulted by the media for expert interviews and has made numerous appearances on TV, radio and in the national press. Steve is also a popular speaker who has made presentations at functions and conferences in Europe, Australia, Asia, Africa and North America.

DR CHRIS SHAMBROOK

Chris Shambrook has been part of the support team for the highly successful GB Rowing Team since 1997 and has worked with multiple World Championship winning crews. In addition, Chris was a key member of the support team for the Men's Eight that won Gold at the Sydney Olympic Games – the first British crew to claim this blue-riband prize since 1912. Chris also works with the Cambridge University Boat Race crews and in recent times has provided support to Nick Faldo's hand-picked 'Team Faldo' squad, working alongside Nick and the support team. Chris is also a consultant to the England and Wales Cricket Board and has provided consultancy to four different county academies as well as the National Academy. Within football, Chris was a member of the team that contributed to the development of the FA's inaugural Diploma in Sport Psychology and has provided support to Sunderland AFC in the past, as well as a number of individual players from the Premiership and the Nationwide Leagues.

Dedications

To my supporters club at home . . . Morgan who will next season be playing soccer in Canada; Alexa, our very own DQ; and Donna who makes it all possible.

Steve Bull, 2004

This book is dedicated to my family . . . Ma and Pa for allowing me to pursue my passion in sport and guiding me along the way. Most importantly to Jules and Jasmine – your support and patience while this was written has been so needed and is so appreciated.

Chris Shambrook, 2004

Natural talent is a great starting point but from personal experience I know that learning to perform is absolutely vital – every aspect of performance, including the mental aspect must be just right if potential is to be fulfilled. In that respect this book is a 'must read' for players at all levels who are serious about performing their best – I certainly use many of the techniques in my daily preparation.

David James, England Goalkeeper

In the afternoon we gathered the 65 finalists (of the Faldo Series players) together for a question and answer session on the range. Some of the questions were mine. 'How many of you have read a sport psychology book?', I asked. Amazingly there was a show of just three hands. 'That's pathetic,' I chided, 'you've got to start reading.'

Preparation is the most important lesson they must learn. They've got to understand they have committed to their discipline. They've got to programme their body and mind for the Sunday they wake up leading a tournament. What people don't realise when they see me sitting at breakfast wearing my 'cold' and 'aloof' blank face is that I am already in golf mode. I'm already in the starting blocks and planning my day.

Nick Faldo, six times Major Winner and Britain's greatest ever golfer
(*The Sunday Times*, 7/9/03)

This quote by Nick Faldo, and taken from the Faldo Series website, may not be about football or footballers but we are convinced of its relevance. It highlights the importance of being mentally prepared for competition and suggests that 'reading' is an essential part of this process.

In this book we have attempted to demystify sport psychology and present a set of mental skills tools in a practical and user-friendly manner.

We are confident that as you read the book you will find many different tips and techniques that will prove useful in your training, preparation and performance.

Whether you play for the local pub side or a Premiership club, there is something in here for you. We hope you enjoy 'the read'!

To Start . . .

This book will take you through a 7-Step Plan designed to improve your mental toughness. Before beginning the plan though, we think it would be useful for you to spend a few minutes considering how you would rate yourself on each of the skills covered in the 7 Steps. Below is a profiling wheel that summarizes each of the skills you will learn about. It serves as a good summary of the book as well.

Rate yourself by shading in the score that you would give yourself right now on each skill. It may be worth getting a coach or team-mate to rate you as well so that you can compare scores.

This is a profile chart that you could revisit in the future when you've learnt all the skills and have practised them for a while.

When you've finished rating yourself, you're ready to start the book . . .

Winning Mind Profile

INTRODUCTION

Winning Minds

Preparation is everything. Focus is the key. The concentration has to be exactly right. It's easy to battle it out on the pitch without having prepared fully and then say 'I gave it my all'. ***The point is that if you had prepared carefully you would have had more to give and you'd have played better . . .*** *Winning is too important to take risks. Every minute detail that can make a victory possible has to be attended to. That's the difference between winning and losing.*

Eric Cantona (*Cantona on Cantona*, 1996)

Whether in the media, or in coaching seminars, the place of mental preparation for sport is becoming increasingly recognized as a variable that can make the difference between success and failure – whatever your level. With individuals and teams very often matched on physical, technical and tactical factors, it is often left to less thoroughly prepared factors such as attitude, focus and belief, to make the telling difference at critical performance moments.

Much is written about how to physically prepare players to achieve the peak of their fitness. Volumes exist focusing upon how to coach the key skills and tactics required to be a successful individual or team. However, when it comes to specific, focused advice that outlines how we can systematically develop the mental skills and attitudes that produce a 'winning mind', there is still relatively little structured information available for coaches and players alike. It is interesting that when it comes to the mental side of the game, players and teams wait for psychological 'problems' to present themselves before they think about fixing them. If this approach were taken with other elements of effective preparation, then players would wait to become unfit before they started doing fitness training, and would only do tactical and skill training when it was clear that skills had broken down, and tactics were not being employed properly. So . . . if we achieve nothing else with this book, we want every reader to go away with the idea that 'Mental Fitness' can be developed, and that we should not be waiting for players to become mentally 'unfit' before we start teaching them about how to improve their mental abilities to cope with the various preparation and playing demands of the game.

Ask yourself . . .

- How 'mentally fit' are you or your players at the moment?
- Have you done the equivalent of pre-season 'mind' training to provide a sound base to your mental fitness components?
- Are you working on maintaining and improving your or your players' 'mental performance'?

Our aim with this book is to provide some clear, common-sense, football-focused advice that will build a strong foundation for the key

> Football is a simple game. The hard part is making it look simple.
>
> **Ron Greenwood**
> Former England Manager
> (In Pickering, *Great Sporting Quotations*, 2000)

mental skills that are required by individual players, and teams. Once the foundation is in place, it is obviously a lot easier for players and coaches to maintain greater consistency in attitude and thinking . . . and in our experience, the most successful performers that we have observed and worked with have very consistent approaches to key factors such as their self-belief, concentration style, stress management, optimistic attitude and motivation. It is no surprise that with these consistent attitudes and mental skills, consistent performances follow close behind.

We will be striving to help you develop a *consistent* foundation to your 'mind training' and how well your mind will perform during matches.

START WITH THE END IN MIND . . .

In order to kick off on the right foot, we need to bring into view the final goals that we are striving for in relation to the mental side of the game. More often than not, coaches and players talk about the importance of 'mental toughness' when discussing the psychology of playing. As this is such a frequently used term within sport, and something that is accepted as being required to really get the most from a performer, 'mental toughness' is a good place for us to start. If we want players to be mentally tough, what does this really mean? What does mental toughness consist of? What kind of things can you do to help someone develop their mental toughness?

Most people in sport, if given enough time and competitive opportunities, will use and practise mental skills on their own because they find that by doing so their performances are more consistent. However, most performers do not have the luxury of unlimited time and competitive opportunities. They cannot afford to spend several seasons learning mental lessons and skills as they take a trial and error approach to building their mental toughness. Even five-time Olympic Gold Medallist Sir Steve Redgrave wishes he had been given the opportunity to develop specific mental skills earlier in his career, and he is not alone as a highly successful athlete who feels he could have been performing at an even higher level earlier in his career if he had been taught the mental skills rather than having had to learn them the hard way.

> I had been developing ideas like that (mental skills) myself, naturally over the years. It would have been useful if someone had told me seven or eight years before, at the start of my career . . . It takes a considerable period of time to develop natural sporting mental skills.
>
> **Sir Steve Redgrave**
> (*A Golden Age – The Autobiography*, 2000)

As we begin to outline the importance of mental toughness, you will begin to appreciate how the skills and specific topics in the follow-up chapters help to bring to life some of the broad ideas introduced through the notion of mental toughness. Therefore, the remainder of this chapter will outline key components of mental toughness that can be worked on, and in the specific later chapters of the book, you will see how to improve abilities within the separate areas of the mental toughness equation.

WHAT IS MENTAL TOUGHNESS?

As a result of the applied work and research in which we've been engaged throughout our careers as sport psychologists, we have developed some clear recommendations that can be made relating to the factors behind mentally tough performers (interestingly, these attributes apply to coaches as well as players, and we also see that they exist within the business environments within which we work). We have seen these characteristics displayed time and time again by the most successful performers, and they are equally applicable for footballers who want to fulfil their potential.

> I knew our time was almost up. I looked around and I saw the cup being carried down to the pitch with Bayern Munich colours on it. Two minutes later, I had it in my own hands, and it was ours.
>
> **David Beckham**
> (*The Times*, 28/5/99)

MENTAL TOUGHNESS ATTRIBUTES

Within sport psychology research, there are actually dozens of mental characteristics that have been associated with being mentally tough. Within this chapter, we have chosen the top five characteristics that we have identified within our own work and research as being consistently important across all sports. These characteristics should give you a good sense of the kinds of attitudes and thinking skills that we need to be promoting within training environments. If players can begin to develop and exploit these winning mind components through their training, then there is a great opportunity to ensure that mind and body development is synchronized, and players experience 'total' preparation.

1. Robust Self-Confidence

Mentally tough players have a real sense of self-belief. They are extremely confident and believe they have the capacity to play consistently well under the most challenging situations. They also *do* produce the goods consistently, so don't confuse this with players who think they are superb, but only deliver from time to time, and actually possess a misplaced sense of self-belief! For players with robust self-confidence, if a game is not going well, they have the ability to remain positive and focused on producing an individual performance that will provide the best chances of turning the game around. Their robust self-belief allows them to stay positive throughout, focused on playing to their strengths, and determined to leave the pitch at the end of the game knowing they gave themselves and the team the best possible chance of turning things around. It is an obvious point to raise, but if these players are able to focus on playing to their strengths, then by definition they know and value what those strengths are. It is easy to expect players to know what they are good at, but as you will see later in the book, concerted efforts have to be made to ensure that players spend the time defining their strengths, as all too often this is an obvious area of performance psychology that is not exploited.

On an individual level, you need look no further than David Beckham in the final World Cup qualifying game against Greece in 2001 at Old Trafford for a great example of the robust self-confidence attribute. Beckham's tireless work-rate demonstrated the unshakeable self-confidence that eventually England would gain the required result. Equally, with each free kick Beckham took, he stepped up with the same level of belief that he was going to score. Previous unsuccessful attempts had not dented his concrete belief that he would score each time he placed the ball for the next effort. Beckham truly has robust belief about his ability as a player that significantly contributes to his mental toughness.

It's interesting to note that another characteristic we associate with mentally tough

Robust Confidence Role Models

Name your top three players who you believe to possess robust self-confidence?
1. 2. 3.

What behaviours do they show from day to day and in matches that directly result from this type of self-belief?

Which of these behaviours do you feel you, or your players, could benefit from improving?

performers is the 'never-say-die' attitude Beckham consistently exhibits in matches. With self-belief not waning, the 'never-say-die mindset' really makes sure that every possible opportunity for success is taken. The 'never-say-die' approach is not just switched on during matches, but is usually part of the day-to-day training mindset of the player too – therefore, whether we are talking about fitness work, or rehabilitation from injury, the mentally tough players stay true to this work ethic every day. It is therefore unsurprising that they can use this thinking style so effectively when it really counts in matches.

We have seen many performers who appear to have *high* self-confidence, but actually when put under pressure, self-doubts emerge and performance suffers – their self-confidence is not robust, yet they have a superficial high self-confidence, but when things are not going well, effort and concentration will drop off and performance will suffer. *They let the situation control them*, rather than maintaining the belief that they have the ability to control the situation by performing to their strengths. Interestingly, mentally tough players will have the self-doubts too, but these doubts are usually used to help fuel the determination to ultimately succeed. As the old cliché goes, *'let your attitude determine your performance in a match, not the other way around.'*

From the mental toughness perspective then, the importance of robust self-confidence shows us how critical it is to help players *build* their confidence in the right way, by creating strong foundations. Most approaches to confidence-building try to create short-cuts to helping a player believe in themselves more. These can work in the short term, but will not ultimately result in a mentally tough player. These players will always rely on the external, quick-fix, injections of artificial confidence to give themselves some momentary belief that is very prone to disappear just at the crucial moment! To help develop robust self-confidence, a longer-term approach to confidence needs to be taken. **Step 2** outlines some of the key techniques that players can use to help establish the strong foundation to begin with, and then, more importantly, the approaches that can be used to help *maintain* the strong confidence once it has been constructed. The process takes time, but interestingly, mentally tough performers will not be put off knowing that they have to work hard to achieve their aim of robust confidence!

As a start-up exercise, spend a few minutes completing the box above. This should give you some idea on which to begin working.

2. Good Decision-Making Under Pressure

As you'll see, mental toughness has general components about preparing for performing, and it also has specific components that are all

> Playing for England is like a game of chess. It's not cut and thrust like the premiership. If you give the ball away at international level, you don't see it again for five minutes.
>
> **Teddy Sheringham**
> (*The Daily Telegraph*, 27/5/98)

about how mentally tough players think within a match. 'Good decision-making under pressure' is a quality that we repeatedly see in the great players, and the great performers in all sports. Their ability to make the right decision at the right time is no accident – it results from the quality of their preparation.

Good decision-making under pressure can be seen in the players who remain calm, and focused on what needs to be done, during the key periods of a match. They can clearly make good decisions about what is and isn't important when others around them might be focused on things that are happening that are not within their control, or that are not really critical to the outcome of the game. Under pressure, many players begin to focus on issues that are out of their control. They begin to argue with officials, they might begin to focus more on winning a personal battle with a specific opposing player rather than staying focused on what needs to be achieved for the team. Mentally tough players stay focused on the things over which they have control. In short, mentally tough players remember the old sport psychology adage 'control the controllables'. Rather than perhaps thinking about 'good decision-making under pressure'; it is helpful to think of this characteristic as 'not making bad decisions under pressure'. You don't really notice the truly mentally tough players making good decisions, because you accept that these are going to be the kind of players who give you consistent performances and seem naturally to do the right thing at the right time. These players don't actually make bad decisions under pressure. They don't rashly dive in, they don't give the ball away at critical moments, they don't get involved in off-the-ball incidents, they don't drift out of the game, they don't argue with officials. They do give you a sense of confidence, control, assuredness and optimism when they are on the ball. As with all of the mental toughness characteristics, you should see these qualities as being on a continuum. Therefore, it's not an all-or-nothing thing. You will see a full range of abilities, and the true test of this quality is to observe *how consistently* players show good decision-making under pressure. Look at the scale below, and see if you can identify how good you, or your key players, are on this component.

The players who don't make the bad decisions under pressure don't let the situation they are in change their thinking. Whether they are defender, goalkeeper, midfielder or attacker, they stay focused on

Consistently makes poor decisions and loses focus under pressure.	Shows more bad than good decision-making.	Evenly balanced between good and bad decision-making.	Shows more good than bad decision-making. Needs to eradicate the few bad decisions.	Consistently makes good decisions and remains focused on things that matter.

their role, and what they need to do in their position to keep the shape of the team, and ensure that the right tactics are being employed. These players will use the pressure of the situation as a positive reminder of what they need to do and how they need to do it. The concentration chapter later in the book will act as a strong source of information for how to develop this ability in players. If you are going to improve your ability to make decisions under pressure, then you need to practise the various kinds of exercises that are introduced in **Step 4**.

3. Self-belief in Making the Difference

Although this is another confidence-related factor, it is an important mental toughness factor in its own right. Mentally tough performers in team sports repeatedly feel that the team is a better team when their name is on the team-sheet. These players justifiably believe that they have specific physical, technical, tactical and mental characteristics that positively add to the performance of the team. They do not necessarily show this belief off to everyone, as often, actions will speak louder than words for them. These players also believe that they can make a difference at critical times, so would be willing to put themselves forward in pressure situations to be the one who will make the telling pass, take possession at critical moments to control the game, or step forward to slot away the winning penalty.

> For me, Beckham would come into the Eric Cantona category, a player who leads by example on the field. Cantona had a great presence on the field and was a scorer of important goals. Similarly, David impresses me by his example on the field. He never stops running, he plays with supreme confidence, he always tries his hardest and he scores important goals.
>
> **Sir Alex Ferguson**
> (In Balchover & Brady, *The 90 Minute Manager*, 2002)

> I knew Michael would be ready to take the penalty himself. 'Do you want me to have it?' 'No. I'm having it.' And I was there, the ball in my hand, putting it down on the spot.
>
> **David Beckham** (describing the seconds before he famously kicked the penalty against Argentina in the 2002 World Cup)
> (*David Beckham: My Side*, 2003)

Therefore, players who have a strong self-belief that they make the difference will be happy to take responsibility on board. As the pressure grows, they become more visible, and more involved in the game . . . they do not hide away. This is closely linked to the positive body language that is associated with mentally tough performers, and is an area that you will see referred to at various times throughout this book. One of the best examples of this kind of self-belief is demonstrated in the player who is the first to volunteer to take a penalty in the penalty shoot-out. These players have a strong resolve and relish the chance of winning the game for their team. Compare this with the attitude of a player who is reluctant to step forward and volunteer to take the penalty for fear of failing.

This self-belief often comes from having a very clear understanding of their roles and responsibilities in the team, and a very clear understanding that they possess a unique set of abilities that will allow them to carry out the role better than anyone else. Once again, their toughness comes from knowing themselves as a player, and knowing what they have to offer a team. This highlights the importance of some of the ideas relating to team-work that will be introduced in **Step 6**, and even though the focus is on the team, there is an important individual focus too.

We have seen players of this kind work on developing this self-belief by making sure that they regularly and honestly reflect on their performances in training and matches. Their honest self-appraisal helps them to have a very clear understanding of what they have to offer any team. Too often, players with similar abilities do not possess the same level of belief because rather than working out for themselves why as a player they have more to offer than someone else, they rely upon coaches, other players, or the media to tell them what they should believe in. Once again, **Step 2** will help to outline some of the key tips that can be used to encourage players to build up their own, consistent sources of self-confidence.

4. Thrive on Competition with Yourself as Well as Others

Mentally tough performers have a really positive attitude towards competition – both with themselves and with other people. Mentally tough performers look forward to the opportunity to compete, and they see the pressure of competition as something to look forward to. After all, the competition time is the reason for all the hard work and preparation, so the mentally tough performers see this as an opportunity to shine, rather than as a threatening situation. The mentally tough players really have an insatiable drive to succeed, and be the best they can possibly be, as well as collect the trophies and titles that they know their talent warrants.

When the competition is at its toughest, this is when the mentally toughest players are prone to rise to the occasion, and produce the most memorable performances. In recent times, the performances of Zinedine Zidane in World Cup and European Cup finals have been telling examples of the mentally tough player stepping up to the challenge. From further back in football history, another great example would be Bobby Moore's performance for England versus Brazil in the 1970 World Cup Finals. In this game, when the individual and team competition was of the highest level, Moore produced a performance that is still talked about today for its quality and consistency. As well as rising to the occasion like this, you will recognize mentally tough performers for the consistent level of quality they produce week in, week out, and much of this performance consistency is produced as a result of their attitude towards competing with themselves.

The mentally toughest players we have seen have set themselves strict levels of achievement for practice, so that they are effectively competing with their own standards and expectations. Successfully achieving these personally set standards obviously allows these players to develop a strong sense of progress in their game, and more importantly, gives them very important standards to strive for in matches. These players are world class at 'playing like they train, and training like they play'. This philosophy is actually about the quality of work carried out, and being able to switch into the appropriate mindset, producing high levels of concentration in training when it's time to work. Mentally tough players will build a lot of confidence from competing with themselves, and this will give them the confidence springboard that they need to compete against the opposition in the knowledge that they have prepared as thoroughly as possible to play to their potential. Many other players see competition and training as two completely separate commodities, and by not competing with themselves effectively in training, these players do not have the same conviction that they will be able to produce a really effective performance when they need one.

By competing with themselves as well as other people, mentally tough performers:

1. Know how good they are, and know what they have to offer as a player. They know they are good enough to play at

the level to which they are currently committed.

2. They know what they need to focus on in order to get a good performance out of themselves.

3. They can trust that they will be able to produce a really great performance when they need one.

Looking at numbers 1, 2, and 3 above, where would you put yourself, or your players, on the *hoping to knowing* continuum?

Hoping ◄·································► Knowing

If players are towards the k*nowing* end on all three points, then they are usually more consistent, independent and effective players. In our experience, we see many people in the top levels of sport who would score high on *knowing* for number 1, that is, they know they are good enough and have the abilities to perform at their current level. However, few players take the time, early in their careers, to truly work out their answers for numbers 2 and 3, that really give them the knowledge to be in control of their performance level when they most need it. With the right approach, and the introduction of consistent 'mental fitness' training, we believe that players can get a head start in their careers by making sure they are towards the knowing end of the continuum for all three questions.

Without a positive attitude towards improving your own standards, or towards exploiting competitive opportunities, it can take a long time for players to learn the necessary information that helps them move from 'hoping' to 'knowing'. The later chapters in the book will highlight some key ways in which goals can be used to maximize this learning, and also how the pressure of big competitions can be managed to increase the likelihood of players 'playing like they train'.

5. 'Go the Extra Mile' and Make Sacrifices Mindset

We've already outlined in the previous section that mentally tough performers have a huge drive to be the best, and a desire to succeed that helps to set them apart from other performers. The competitiveness that they have with themselves allows them to develop a very strong 'go the extra mile' mindset. These players are great at working out what needs to be achieved, and how it needs to be achieved in order that they have the best chance of success. Therefore, the 'go the extra mile' mindset is synonymous with the quality preparation that we know is essential for performing at the very highest level . . . repeatedly. Mentally tough players will spend the extra time that it takes to make sure that they get expert at doing ordinary things to an extraordinary level. It is very easy not to go the extra mile. It is very easy to finish practice when the formal structured session finishes – the mentally tough players very clearly see how they will benefit in the short term, but more importantly in the long term, by putting in small, but highly significant amounts of individual effort.

There are many small behaviours in sport that can add up over time to make a significant difference. Sticking with these behaviours over time takes mental toughness, and trusting that doing the right things, repeatedly, will pay off takes great discipline and bloody-mindedness.

> Some athletes have this wonderful ability to always win. It's as though it's a natural state of mind.
>
> **Sven-Goran Eriksson**
> (*Sven-Goran Eriksson on Football*, 2002)

> As his team-mates were vanishing from the pitch at the Cliff, he approached me and asked if he could have the assistance of two players. 'What for?' I asked. 'To practise', he replied. That took me back. It was not exactly a standard request. I was naturally delighted to accede to Eric's wishes and quickly provided him with two young players and a goalkeeper so that he could spend half an hour practising volleys. Meanwhile, the players who had gone indoors at the Cliff were realizing that Cantona had not come back in and before long they knew why. At the end of training the next day, several of them hung around to join in the practice with Eric, and it is now an integral part of our regime. Many people have justifiably acclaimed Cantona as a catalyst who had a crucial impact on our successes while he was with the club but nothing he did in matches meant more than the way he opened my eyes to the indispensability of practice. Practice makes players.
>
> **Sir Alex Ferguson**
> (*Managing My Life*, 1999)

> A young player comes into the game, looks the part. He's not a drinker, looks after himself. Then, as soon as he gets into the first team, he thinks that to show he's a man he has to drink. In probably every other country, the young player actually becomes more serious about the game. He'll do anything he can to improve and stay in the team . . . The problem here is that players think they can drink. Maybe they could once, but the game demands so much more now, not just physically but mentally because of greater tactical awareness. If you drink, you lose half an inch, then an inch, then half a yard, then a yard and your brain also becomes gradually slower to react. And in the process you lose the chance to progress from being a Premiership player to a top-class player. I compare top-class players to racing cars. Drinking alcohol is as silly as putting diesel in a racing car . . . If you have a booze-up every week, you won't edge out a foreign player who doesn't.
>
> **Geràrd Houllier**
> (*The Sunday Telegraph*, 13/2/00)

When Daley Thompson was competing at his peak in the Decathlon he made a point of training on Christmas Day, because he knew his opponents would be tucking into a large dinner, and not sticking with their normal training schedule. This was the attitude that took Thompson to great success . . . and this is just the kind of attitude that for modern footballers is even harder to engender. Daley Thompson didn't get extra money for training smarter and harder than his opponents, but he did get the intrinsic satisfaction and knowledge that he was doing everything possible to fulfil his potential as an athlete. Here was a truly professional attitude and mindset in a sport that was far from professional at the time in terms of financial reward. Professional attitude is a commodity that needs to be harnessed much more effectively in football in an era when professional earnings can easily get in the way of a player's true motivation for playing.

In relation to the 'making sacrifices' element of this characteristic, players have to make strong decisions about how they are going to manage their careers. For the duration of a sporting career, there are various social and lifestyle choices that need to be made in order that players give themselves the best chance of succeeding. Players need to make strong choices that relate to how they are going to give their mind and body the best possible chance of reaching and maintaining peak fitness levels – for the duration of their careers. This might mean specific lifestyle sacrifices, while they are playing, but mentally tough performers are very good at making and keeping a commitment to these key behaviours that will ultimately give them a performance edge. Because the mentally tough performers know that these sacrifices are performance focused, and also restricted to the portion of their life when they are performing, they see these sacrifices as positive and manageable choices, that is, they remain in control by recognizing that they have chosen to make a specific sacrifice that will ultimately benefit them. Players who perhaps don't have the mental toughness required to get to, and remain at the very top for extended periods of time, would see the sacrifices as being forced upon them, and something that they begrudge having to make. Such subtle differences in attitude once again reinforce the importance of the mind, and understanding how we need to take control of the mind in order truly to get close to fulfilling potential.

Steve McClaren led Middlesborough to their first ever domestic trophy in 2004 – McClaren has fully embraced sport psychology as an essential component of his managerial approach. © EMPICS

The ability to make sacrifices and stick to them, as well as perceive them positively, is often dependent on the short, medium and long-term view that the players have of themselves. You will see in the goal-setting information later in the book, that we would encourage players to develop a long-term view of what they are trying to achieve in the game, and how they are trying to achieve it. Without this kind of planning, it's very easy for players to focus only on the next few days, or the next game, and never really develop a view of how the repeated sacrifices, and repeated 'extra miles', will actually add up to help fulfil potential at a point in the future. Football is a very short-term focused, reactive sport, and because players are going to live in this kind of culture, it is even more important that they carry out the individual planning to help them exploit the 'going the extra mile' mindset all the more effectively through their careers.

> McLaren's whole coaching philosophy is based on the constant striving for individual and collective excellence and the rejection of complacency. This applies even to himself. Few coaches have analysed the psychology of winning as deeply as McLaren. He cites books written by American professional coaches Pat Riley and Bill Walsh as having had a major impact on his coaching career. He has also studied videos and read transcripts of interviews with Michael Jordan, the greatest modern-day basketball player, and studied the coaching techniques employed by his team, the Chicago Bulls. His library on his specialist subject of winning is apparently still growing.
>
> **Bolchover and Brady** in *The 90 Minute Manager*

DEVELOPING DIFFERENT TYPES OF MENTAL TOUGHNESS

During the last few years, we have conducted research on mental toughness and, in addition to the characteristics described earlier, we have uncovered three distinctly different types, each of which relates to football. As you read about these contrasting types of mental toughness, consider how the top five characteristics we have just been discussing might help with improving your mental strength in each of the contexts outlined.

My current rating for 'endurance athlete toughness':

1	2	3	4	5	6	7	8	9	10
Very poor				Average			Very strong		

How could I improve my mental toughness in this area?

1. Endurance Athlete Toughness

This represents a type of toughness associated with extremely arduous training regimes such as those of Olympic rowers, swimmers and distance runners. Training several times a day for most days of the year requires significant lifestyle sacrifices. These performers demonstrate the highest levels of commitment whereby they must almost put their personal and social lives 'on hold' until they have achieved their sporting goals. They have the mental strength to push themselves to their physical limits in training as well as in competition. Their capacity to squeeze out every drop of energy during a physical performance is remarkable.

Football Examples:

- Sticking to a really physically demanding fitness regime during the pre-season period.
- Pushing yourself to keep running as hard as possible during the second period of extra-time when your body is aching to stop.

2. 'Final Putt' Toughness

Making a putt on the 18th green to win a golf match requires a very different type of mental toughness from the Olympic rower's approach. Any golf fan will associate with the challenge of sinking the 'big putt' and may be able to contemplate the demands of holing from 6 foot to win the Ryder Cup or a 'Major'. This is all about 'holding your nerve' at the critical moments. It requires performers to remain in control of their emotions and execute the motor skills necessary to complete a task. Failure to do this is often referred to as 'choking'. It requires a completely different mindset from pushing yourself hard in training.

Football Examples:

- Holding your nerve to execute the penalty kick at a critical time that you know will determine the result of the match.
- Staying calm and in control when collecting the ball knowing that you are the last line of defense and you must make a clearance to avoid conceding a certain goal.

Sven-Goran Eriksson, unsurprisingly, was equally full of praise for his inspirational skipper. 'I think he was very happy,' the coach said. 'You could see it afterwards. He is not 100% fit yet. He has no problem with the foot but he needs games. To take a penalty when it's nil–nil once again showed that he's a good captain. Mentally he's extremely strong.

The *Guardian* newspaper

My current rating for 'final putt toughness':

1 2 3 4 5 6 7 8 9 10
Very poor Average Very strong

How could I improve my mental toughness in this area?

My current rating for 'Atherton–Donald toughness':

1 2 3 4 5 6 7 8 9 10
Very poor Average Very strong

How could I improve my mental toughness in this area?

3. 'Atherton–Donald' Toughness

This type of mental toughness acquires its name from the classic encounter between Michael Atherton and Allan Donald in the cricket match between England and South Africa at Trent Bridge in 1998. There was a period of play which lasted less than an hour but which not only influenced the match in question, but also the series as a whole. Donald delivered a series of highly intimidating deliveries to Atherton (and the other batter Nasser Hussain) and the session became a hostile and aggressive battle between two great players. Both players demonstrated the kind of mental toughness necessary to deal with a 'head-to-head' battle in the face of significant hostility and serious consequences regarding match outcome. Maintaining emotional control and effective management of decision-making is crucial in these circumstances

Football Examples:

- Standing up for yourself when being intimidated by the opposition but not being drawn into retaliation.
- Staying focused and making good decisions when a certain player is trying to disrupt your concentration by 'verbal sledging' or hostile tackling.

Developing Superior Mental Preparation

Having read the pages of this chapter, and considered your personal responses to some of the questions in the boxes, you may be asking how you can go about improving specific aspects of your mental approach. The remaining chapters of this book are designed to help you do this. Work your way through the book and consider how you can adapt the mental skills outlined to suit your own individual strengths and weaknesses. You must be prepared though, to spend time developing these skills. Be patient and the improvement will come but don't expect miracles overnight. Superior mental preparation is a skill – and, as such, some people find it easier than others but there is always room for improvement.

Mental skills training does not take the place of physical, technical or tactical training. It enhances these and increases the probability that what is accomplished through these forms of training will be evidenced on match days. Footballers who have good mental skills are able to make pressure work for them. They are able to stay focused at the critical situations during matches. They do not get distracted by errors. They are confident in their ability even when things are going badly. They win matches!

By utilizing the skills outlined in this book, we cannot promise you footballing glory. The correct mental approach is no substitute for basic inherited physical ability. Positive thinking will not make you better than you have the potential to be. But, mental skills training *can, and does*, maximize your chances of getting as close as possible to that potential. It can give you that final edge, those few per cent, which so often mean the difference between winning and losing. In short, if you want to prepare as well as you possibly can, then mental training simply must be a part of that preparation. Remember, it has been said that *'Under pressure you can perform up to 30 per cent better or 30 per cent worse.'*

We are confident that the skills and techniques presented throughout this book will assist you in moving towards the 30 per cent better direction. The rest is up to you!

STEP 1

Taking Aim and Setting Goals

Learning From Outside Football

Setting a goal is not the main thing. It is deciding how you will go about achieving it and sticking with that plan.

Tom Landry, Former American Football Coach

My goal was that I wanted to get better every day. That was a goal I had. So, how do I get better? Well I have to assess what I have to get better at and what I am going to do to get better at it.

Craig Billington, NHL Goalie

We know football is a game all about *scoring* goals, but in this chapter our aim is to get you to focus upon the importance of *setting* goals and targets. Whether it is for individual players, a team or a whole club, the setting and reviewing of goals are the secrets to developing and maintaining confidence, as well as maximizing motivation for all phases of performance.

Goals are essential to success in any walk of life. If we really want to stretch our potential to the limit, we have to set targets that direct, inform and motivate us so that we are maximally committed to our best performance in every training session or match. Setting and using goals is one of the classic areas in sport psychology where the idea is simple, and makes total sense, but it is very hard to actually carry out the process of goal-setting with the required consistency to ensure it is maximally effective – the common sense is not translated into common practice! Therefore, you need to think of goal-setting as an ongoing process that should become part and parcel of the way you train and play. We'll be introducing the cycle of *Set–Do–Review*, to help you have a clear, simple structure for sticking with all the effective elements that form the foundation for successful goal-setting.

If we don't have personal goals that we are aiming for, from a motivation, commitment and concentration point of view, this is just like trying to throw a dart at the bull's-eye on a dart board whilst wearing a blindfold! With the blindfold on, we can see nothing, don't know where we're aiming, so our brain has no information to go on to help us make an effort and then work out how to improve next time – performance is poor and is unlikely to get any better. Take the blindfold off, and now we can have a clear idea of what to aim at, what effort is required, and we can get a sense of progress and learning as we make subsequent attempts. These simple examples result in a straightforward question . . . Are you in the dark when it comes to goal-setting, or can you clearly see your targets?

The main focus of this book is to provide you with ways forward for bringing about systematic mental skills development for football. This means that there has to be a clear identification of *what* needs to be improved. However, if the improvement desired is to take place, there has to be a clear set of reasons *why* the changes are important, and then there has to be an ongoing *commitment* to the various methods that will need to be employed to ensure that the desired results are achieved.

Whether it is psychological training, technical development, building fitness or progressing tactically, all these processes require individuals or teams to be prepared to put in the hard work that it takes to bring about the required improvement – no change or improvement is made without *motivation*.

If motivation is not maintained to keep putting in the required effort to change, then ultimately abilities will not improve, confidence will suffer, and performance will stagnate or drop off.

> The great fallacy is that the game is first and last about winning. It's nothing of the kind. The game is about glory. It's about doing things in style, with a flourish, about going out and beating the other lot, not waiting for them to die of boredom.
>
> **Danny Blanchflower** in 1972
> (In Pickering, *Great Sporting Quotations*, 2000)

KEY TYPES OF GOALS – IT'S NOT ALL ABOUT WINNING!

It is easy to simply call a goal a goal. However, within sport there are important differences in the types of goals we can set, and the different types of goals impact in different ways upon confidence, motivation, anxiety, decision-making and concentration. It's important that you have a good feel for what these different kinds of goals are. You will also notice that not all players set each type of goal, but as a general rule, it is sensible to employ the whole range.

Outcome Goals

Outcome goals are at the heart of sport. It is the quest to be the best, to win championships, cup competitions and matches that are what really motivate people – the reason we get up in the morning! These objective measures of success are what managers, teams and players are remembered for. However, outcomes goals are easy to define, and every team or individual usually aspires to achieve the same outcome successes. Therefore, by being in pursuit of your outcome goals, by definition you are focused upon stopping an opponent achieving that same target. Equally, weather conditions, refereeing decisions and injuries can be influences that are outside your control that result in outcome goals not being achieved. Therefore, on a given day, we can perform to the best of our ability, but other factors mean we 'fail' in relation to our outcome goal. In order to maintain motivation and build confidence, we have to be able to take more away from a competition than simply the result. Outcome goals are definitely the spark that set the fires of motivation burning, but we know the secret to a powerful fire is to keep it burning once the spark has been lit. Therefore, we need fuel for the fire, and this is where *performance goals* and *process goals* come into play.

Before considering the other types of goals, ask yourself whether you know that everyone in your team is in pursuit of the same outcome goal? It's easy to assume that 'of course we're all in this for the same reason'. However, it's vital not to leave these outcome goals down to assumptions. As a team you need to make sure that you are all striving for the same outcome goal, and your individual goals are all being focused towards collective success. Spending an extra couple of hours on the collective setting of goals is well worth the extra quality of training that will result. The same collective goal-setting approach needs to be applied to the performance and process goals too if you are really going to get a team to fulfil its potential.

Performance Goals

For every outcome, there are specific measures that would be associated with that success. For example, to win a championship title a certain amount of points will be required, and therefore a certain number of wins, draws and losses. These benchmark figures can easily be established by looking back at previous seasons and predicting likely standards. Performance goals allow you to start to outline *how* you will go about giving yourself the best possible chance of achieving the *outcome* goals. We are more in control of achieving performance goals, so these form a crucial element of the route towards getting our outcome goals.

With recent developments in the game, it is possible to identify even more specific performance measures that indicate *how* performances are achieved, other than just points or goal difference. Performance analysis systems such as PROZONE and OPTA analyse and record key elements of performance. It is easy to establish targets for performance using the detailed evaluation that is available – so, rather than waiting until after the game to see what the stats tell you what you did, you decide ahead of the game what you want to make the stats look like when the game ends! Based upon the specific strengths of a team, and the specific tactics most suited to exploiting the individual talents available, it should be possible to determine success targets for those areas of performance that you believe to be the most important. For example, the percentage of tackles won/tackles made, the percentage of passes completed successfully in the opponents' half, the percentage of shots on target, or interceptions. You don't even need a sophisticated computer analysis package to help you set goals for and review these kinds of goal. Paper and pencil techniques for recording tactical data can be just as effective, either while the game is being watched live, or perhaps reviewed on video.

It might take some time to get a clear idea of exactly what the statistics need to say for your team, but once you have a good feel for the pattern of your typical statistics, then they can be a really useful source of motivation and feedback. Please don't think we are advocating playing by numbers . . . that is certainly not the case. We are recommending that this approach can really help with specifically identifying *how* you want to play in order to maximize the chances of getting the results you are aiming for. With performance goals, it'll become clear to you that not only do the goals focus the team as a whole, they provide a very clear set of targets for individual players to fulfil in their roles, which will be an essential part of the ideas presented in **Step 7**. Once you know how you want the team to play, and you know what the clear responsibilities are of each player, then you can set targets for that

> I think I have improved every year . . . At the start of the season I set myself goals, areas to work on. Then, after every game, I analyse myself so I know what I have done well and what I need to work on . . .
>
> . . . You play so many games, there is always something to work on.
>
> . . . in previous seasons I have wanted to play central defence because I believe my qualities are better suited to it . . .
>
> . . . Playing at left-back was hard physically – you have to be clever at the back and good going forward. Now I prefer to concentrate on being good at the back and helping to concede fewer goals.
>
> **Michael Silvestre**
> (www.Manchesteronline.co.uk)

EXAMPLE TEAM PROCESS GOALS

- Clear, strong communication in the key five-minute periods of each half.
- We are quick to pressure the ball inside the final third of the pitch.
- Exploit our pace and fitness to keep the pressure on the opposition – defence and attack – the full 90 minutes.
- Get the ball into the front two as early as possible – their strength on the ball needs to be exploited.
- We are as focused and positive in injury time as we are at kick-off . . . whatever the score.

player so they can establish how well they have carried out their role for any given match. These specific performance measures allow you to be able to say more than just 'great game' – they very much give you the substance to make it clear *why* it was such a great game because of what the player or team did.

Process Goals

The final element of the essential goal setting components is the in-game, in-performance set of targets. The Process goals help the players identify what they need to think about and focus on in the game if they are going to have the best chance of reaching their *performance* goal targets. These goals tend not to be easily measured or assessed in football, due to the game being very open and free-flowing. However, an individual player might set personal process goals that focus on ideas such as: chase every ball down – never give up, I'll be the most aggressive in any 50–50 tackle, defensive headers – strong and drive through, positive body language for the full 90 minutes. Therefore, these goals help to identify the key reminders that will help keep the player fully focused on their key roles within the game. Similar kinds of *process* goals can easily be identified for the team as a whole, and any good pre-match team-talk is full of these *process* goals. By going through the goals in advance of the pre-match talk, you make sure everyone fully understands what these goals mean for them, why they are important, and how they will allow the team to be successful.

If we get a clear picture of what kinds of attitudes we want to play with, and what kinds of strengths we are looking to exploit, our mind is then focused on doing the right thing as often as possible. If we do that, we then maximize the chances of winning the battles in the *performance* goals area. If we win the *performance* goal battles, then more often than not, we will get the result we deserve.

On pages 28–31 we've given you four examples of this goal-setting process to help you get a clearer picture. There are team and individual goals for a season, and team and individual goals for a match. We've just picked out some limited performance goals, but you can see how everything links together once you work out *why* you're beginning the specific challenge, *what* you're going to aim to achieve in order to be successful, and *how* you're going to be focused in order to do this. You could obviously have as many *WHY*s, *WHAT*s and *HOW*s as you need, so don't be restricted by the simple graphic we've put together.

We know that due to the nature of football, there will be days when you get the processes and the *performance* goals nailed, but somehow the opposition sneak a lucky goal, so you are left frustrated because the result was not achieved. However, you still have all of the positives to take away from the other goals that have been achieved, *and if you had not set and achieved these process and performance goals, then all you would be left to reflect upon is how unlucky you were, and you have no idea how you lost the game.* We would argue that the teams who claim 'we can't even buy a win at the moment', are focused only on *outcome* goals, and have not paid enough attention to

Team – Season Goals

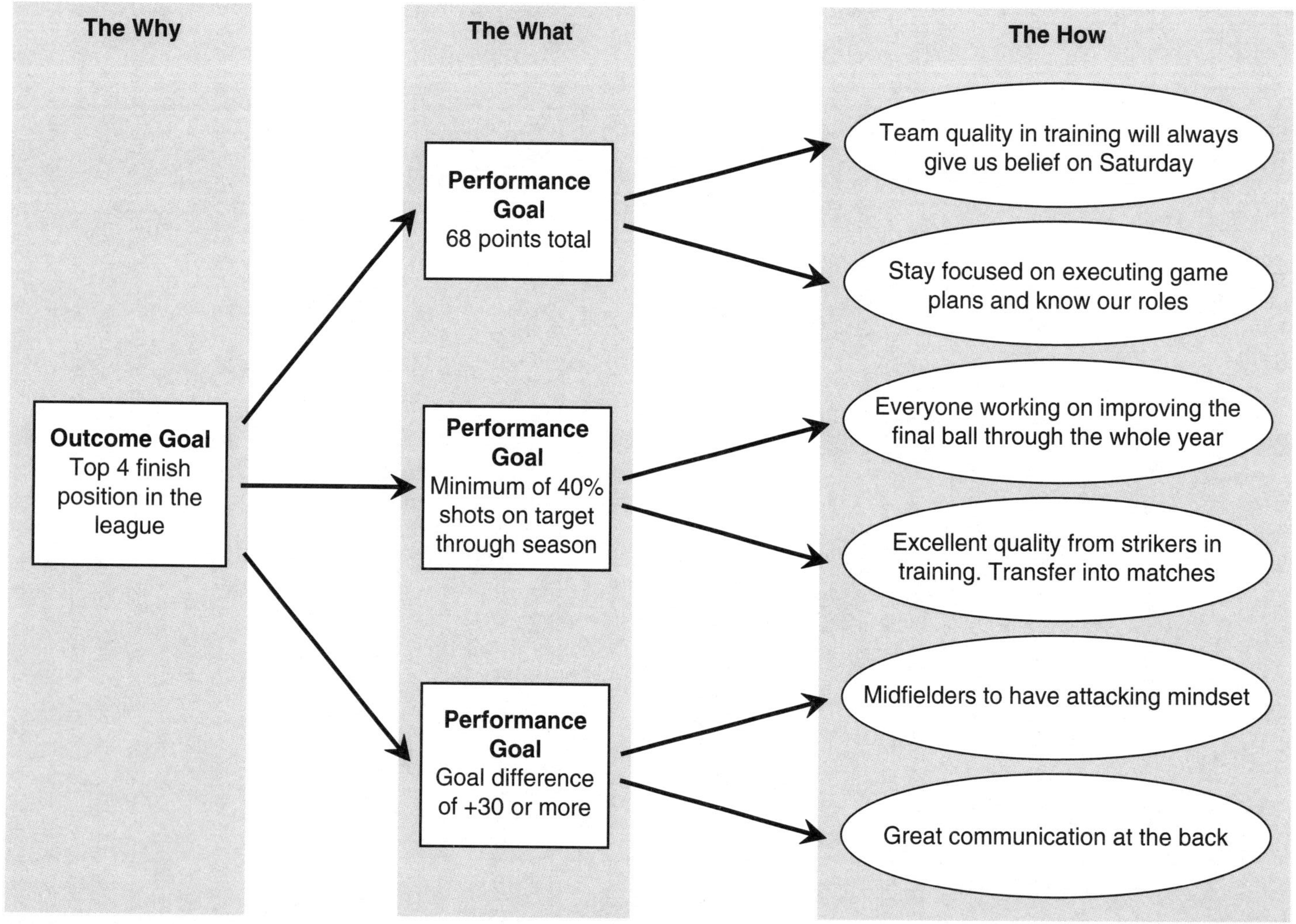

Individual – Season Goals

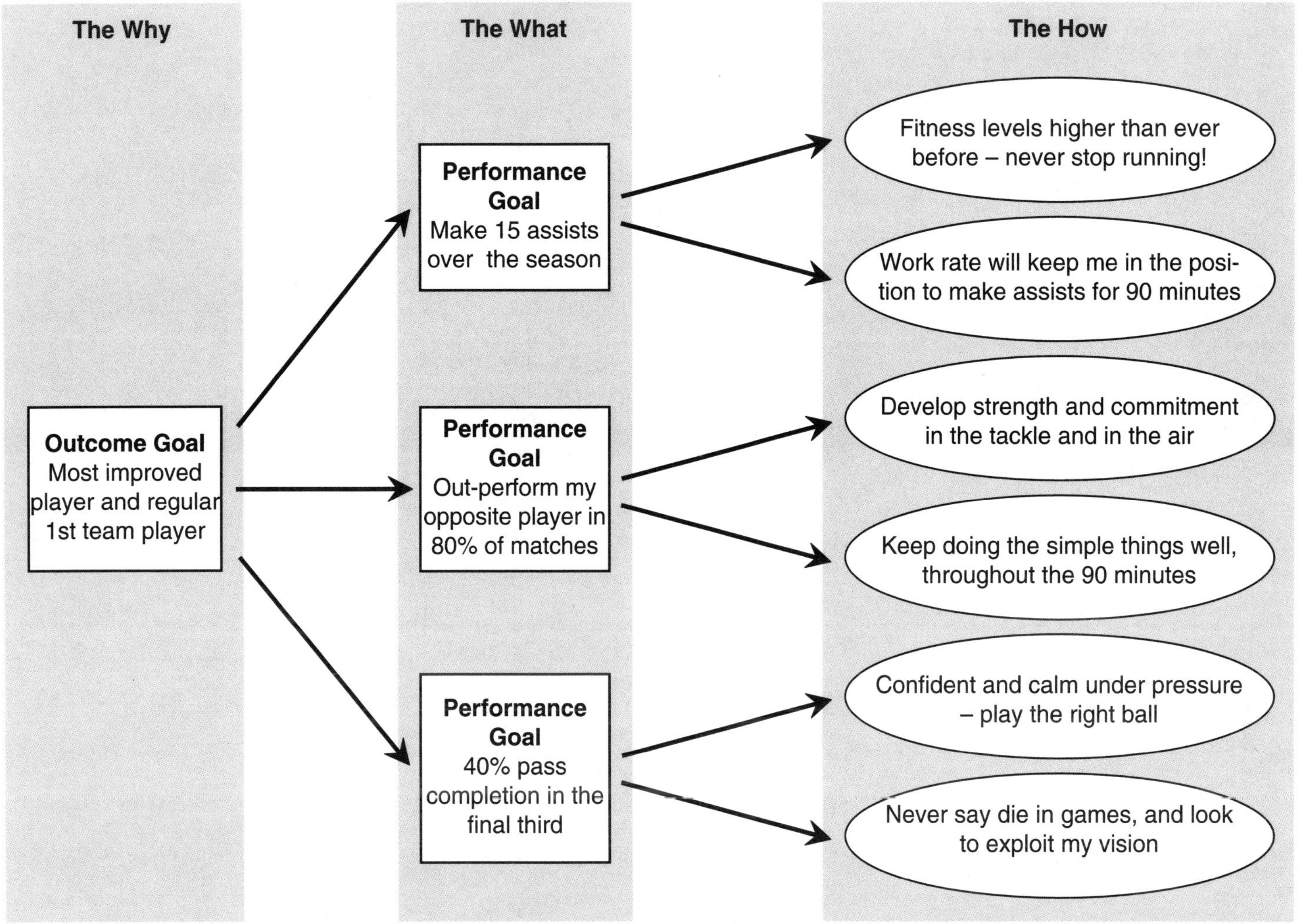

Team – Match Goals

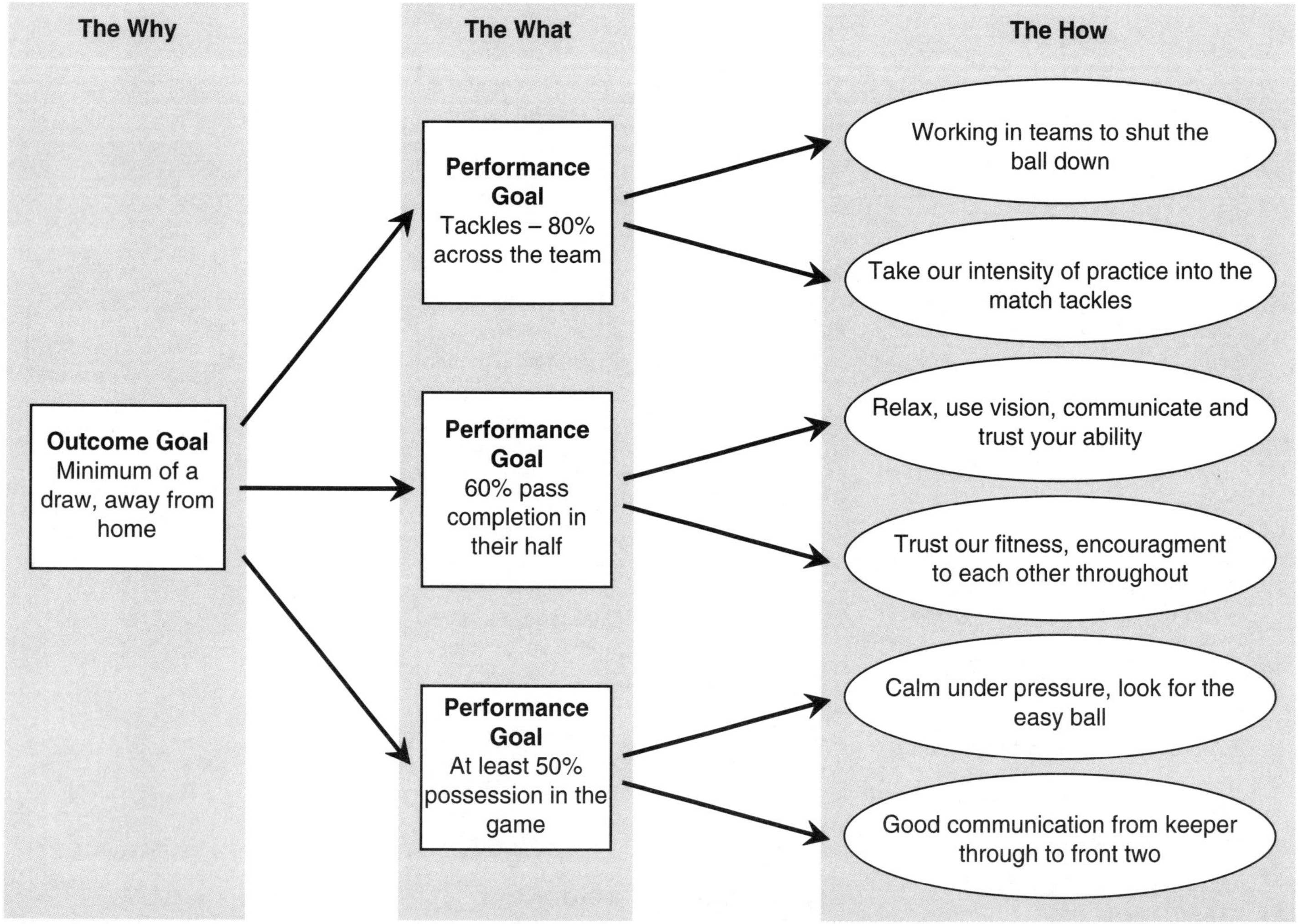

Individual – Match Goals

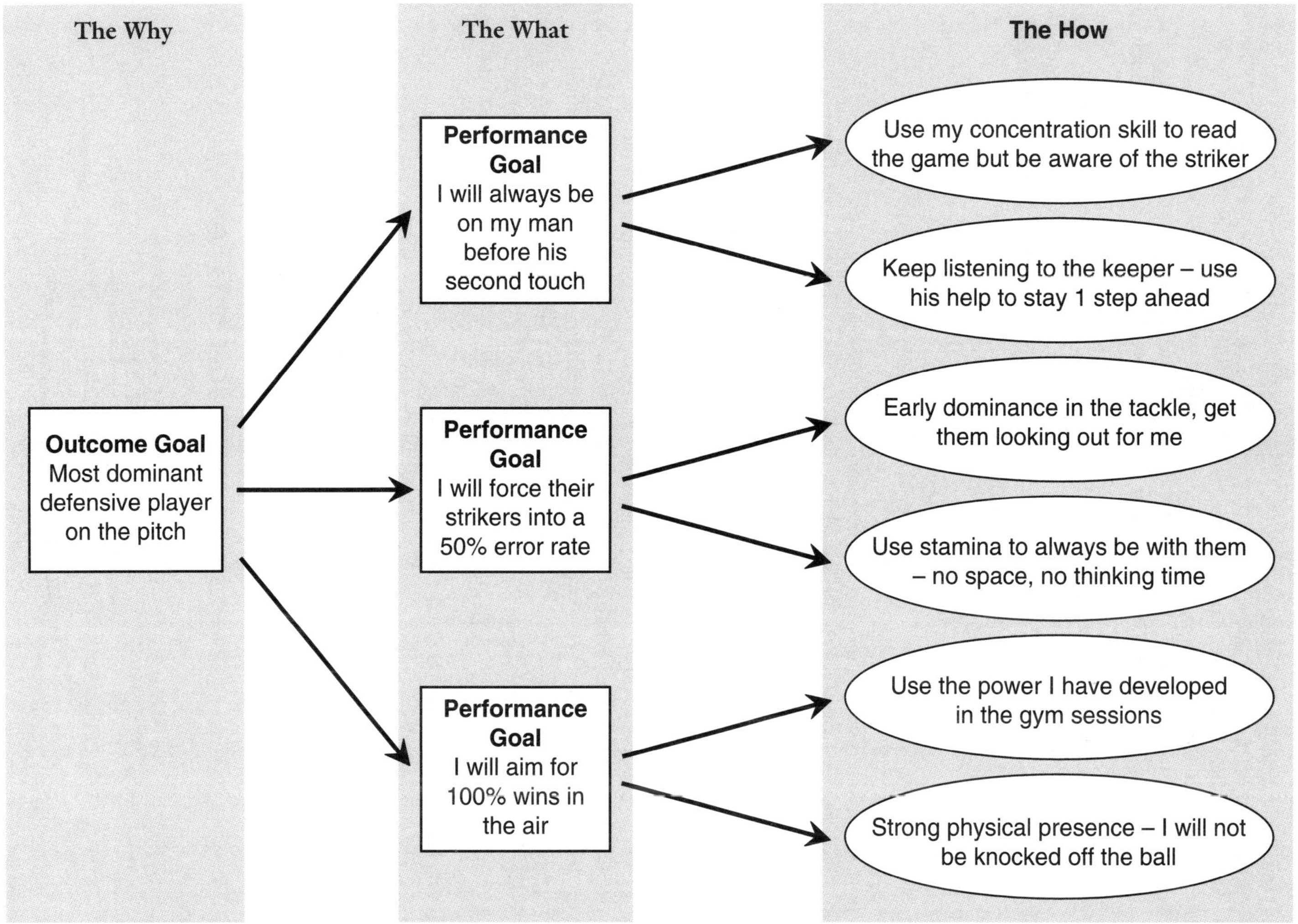

> It's true that we don't concentrate sufficiently on 'learning goals' during training and that we're not very good at following up individual players where these process goals are concerned.
>
> **Sven-Goran Eriksson**
> (*Sven-Goran Eriksson on Football*, 2002)

working out their recipe for maximizing their potential and learning *how* this team produces its best performances (regardless of final score).

And if you don't buy this . . . well there is not a better recent example in the world of sport than the World Cup-winning England Rugby team. Sir Clive Woodward's leadership of this team meant that through their world class use of goal-setting and goal-reviewing, over several years, the team first learnt how to perform, and then learnt how to win.

Remember, as you move down through the three levels in these charts (from Outcome to Process), you are focusing more and more on specific elements of performance over which you have more and more control. This has important implications for both confidence and concentration.

GOOD GOAL-SETTING GUIDELINES

What follows is our simple 3-phase guide to good goal-setting. There's quite a few key points in each phase, but if you follow the phases carefully, you'll end up with all the benefits of a great system. The whole idea is simply based around Set–Do–Review.

If you want a short cut to successful goal-setting, and you want to know which one of the three steps we'd recommend doing more than any other, then we'd say Phase 3 without a doubt! The reasons why that would be our recommendation will become totally clear when you read the next section!

PHASE 1 – SET

Obviously, setting goals is the start of the three steps. There are many great examples of the rules you should try to stick to in order to make sure your goals really work for you, and some of the books in our recommended reading section will outline these for you in detail. In order to get the setting of the goals really spot-on from the outset, we'd argue that you need to make sure that the goals are as meaningful as possible for the team or individual concerned. Therefore, finding a clear process that really works to help set personalized, compelling goals is our first aim for you.

We'd recommend that you invest a good amount of time in the goal-setting process. Too often in sport, coaches and players are so focused on getting on with things, that the planning time is minimized. We'd really recommend that you take the extra time to make sure your goal-setting is as world class as

3 PHASES TO GREAT GOAL SETTING

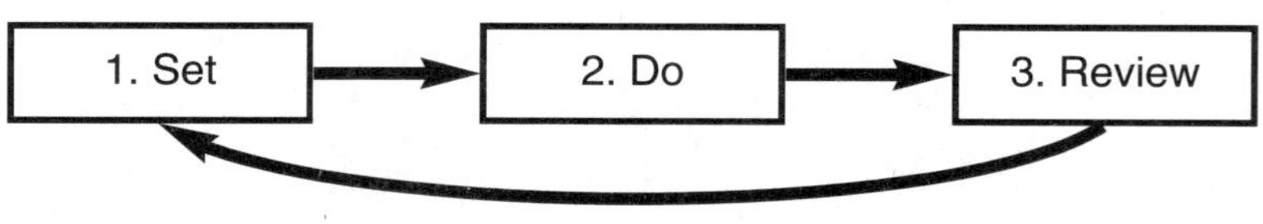

possible, and then when you do start 'getting on with things', they will be carried out with significantly more quality, and will therefore make a bigger difference. If an extra two hours of planning leads to an extra 10 per cent quality of training in the next 200 hours of training, then this is certainly better than rushing the planning, and missing out on extra quality in all of the hours of training that follow – 200 hours of 10 per cent more focused work would make a significant impact on any team!

So, working out which goals are important to a player or the team can be achieved really effectively using a very commonly used approach called Performance Profiling – a technique that has been taken on and used in many different forms within the coaching world. Performance Profiling, for teams or single players, works really well because it starts to make clear all of the different areas that need to be worked upon in order to reach potential.

The process starts by getting the team or individual to consider all of the qualities that go into making up the complete team, or complete player. These qualities are considered under the titles of Fitness; Technique/Skills; Tactics; Mental/Attitudes and Lifestyle. You can see the sample profiles that we've provided to see the kind of things that might come out of the initial brainstorming. These lists can be very long sometimes, but don't be put off by that. You'll also find that depending upon experience, different amounts of qualities will be identified. More is not necessarily better, and it is certainly important from a team perspective to make sure everyone understands what each quality means. This is also worth double-checking even when a player and a coach are completing a profile together. Don't assume you both mean exactly the same thing when you talk about a specific quality. The important thing with the whole process is that the team or player has been included in defining what the important components of performance are – they have not just had a recipe imposed upon them. Because of this involvement, it is more likely that when it comes to improving or developing specific areas, the players will be more motivated to make the changes and put in the work required.

Next, the team or individual rate their level of performance on each quality. If the team or player is to become the finished article, then we could easily assume that they would score 10 out of 10 on each quality, consistently – their average performance would be a maximum score every time! Therefore, with each of the qualities it is important to consider what the average performance is on each one. In this way an honest evaluation has to take place of the 'normal' levels of achievement shown by the team or player. Once each quality has been scored, it is then possible to see which qualities are the strengths of the team or player, and which qualities require bringing into line with the higher scoring qualities.

With a range of qualities and scores it is then possible to target three or four key qualities to work on improving. Players also benefit from identifying three or four qualities that are already strong that they will ensure keep featuring as a performance strength of theirs. Our profiling follow-up form shows how you take the results of the profile and turn them into action.

Once the process has been completed and the goal-setting carried out, you can then schedule in a time for re-profiling to check on progress and ensure that all the qualities are still relevant. Updating the contents and the score for the profile is important, as it keeps players and teams focused on the key issues that will really make a difference at any point in the season.

Quick Step Goal Charts

If you don't want to go through the profiling process, you can simply use the chart format

Performance Profile

Date:

Quality	Score out of 10	Priority area to develop	Priority area to maintain
FITNESS			
Speed over first 5-10 yards	6		
Repeated sprint ability	8		✓
Stamina	8		
Strength	5		
Flexibility	5		
Able to maintain intensity for full 90min	7		
Able to take knocks	5		
TECHNIQUE/SKILLS TACTICS			
First touch	8		
Vision	8		
Passing off both feet	7		
Position awareness	9		✓
Tackling back	8		
Aerial timing	6		
Distance on clearing headers	6		
Reading the game	9		✓
Tracking back	6		
Able to run with the ball out of defence	4	✓	
MENTAL/ATTITUDES			
Calm under pressure	5		
Belief in ability	5		
Stay focused for the full 90min	7		
Never give in	8		✓
Pushing self to always improve	7		
Pre-match preparation	4	✓	
Communication with back four/midfield	6		
LIFESTYLE	4		
Good nutrition		✓	
Stay hydrated	4	✓	
Rest and recovery from training	6		
Minimizing stress outside the game	5		
Well organized for travel.	6		

Profiling Follow-Up

Quality to work on	Action to take	Move score up to this level	Aim to achieve change by... (date)
Able to run ball out of defence	Work on dribbling skills more in training. Bring in pressure training as I improve.	7	The end of pre-season training and pre-season friendlies.
Pre-match preparation	Develop a proper routine that will work home and away. Practise the routine during pre-season friendlies.	8	First match of the season.
Good nutrition	Start eating more balanced meals. Only one take-away per week, more fruit and veg and healthy snacks in the day.	6	3 weeks' time and then set more goals to keep the progress going.
Stay hydrated	Always carry a water bottle with me and take water on the training pitch with me. Keep sipping water through the day.	6	Get the score up within 10 days, and look to be 9/10 by the end of this season.

YOU WILL BE ABLE TO RELY ON YOUR KEY STRENGTHS OF:
Reading the game
Having a never-say-die attitude
Positional awareness
Repeated sprint ability
MAKE SURE THESE GIVE YOU THE CONFIDENCE TO MAKE YOUR IMPROVEMENTS

of goal-setting that we often employ when working one to one with players. With this chart, you simply build up a list of meaningful goals through a detailed discussion that focuses upon all areas of that game that can help to bring about an improved overall game for the player. We always make sure that it's the player's thoughts that are recorded, as once again it's vital that they drive the goal-setting process, and don't have goals imposed upon them. In time, you can use these charts for really effective goals that focus on a block of the season, or a series of matches, maybe even a tournament.

Profiling Follow-Up

Quality to work on	Action to take	Move score up to this level	Aim to achieve change by... (date)

You will be able to rely on your strengths of:

Make sure these give you the confidence to make your improvements

Success!

It's easy to see how you'll be able to use profiling to help you work out whether you have had a successful period of training, or even a match performance. By using each of the qualities, you can establish a score for each quality for a match or training block. If training for the match has been successful, then the qualities will all be at a good level for you – so you could be in a losing team, but personally have good scores on the profile. The disappointment still exists due to the result, but you don't lose sight of a good confidence-building performance in yourself! It's important for individuals and teams to have a clear picture of the many things that success can mean for them, and this approach really helps with that.

CRITICAL TARGETS FOR 2004 SEASON	Name: Date:

The SMARTA System

Set – Do – Review

Skills and tactics training

I will use pre-season training to improve the strength in my left foot when shooting. I'll look to improve power and accuracy week by week through the season – I'll design a test to score myself on in training every two weeks to check progress. By the end of the season this will mean my left foot will be as strong as my right foot.

I will use the pre-match video sessions more effectively to help me improve my readiness for matches. I will write down 2–3 key points to remember with every video we watch.

Fitness training and physical preparation

By the end of the next 6 weeks I'll improve my all-round strength by making a 10% improvement in all of the weights I am lifting in our weights circuit. I'll maintain this level for the rest of the season.

I'll make sure that this season I maintain my position as best I can on the multi-stage fitness test, but I will also improve my score on each test when compared to last season's.

I'll use the physio to help me carry out at least three stretching sessions each week throughout the season – check this goal monthly.

'Training the brain' – attitude and mental skills

I'm going to improve my shooting under pressure this season. Get coach to rate me every month and use visualization to help me 'practise' under pressure.

I will stop letting mistakes break my concentration. I will develop a plan of how to think after an error, and practise it in training and use it in matches. I will look for improvements week by week through the season, and will have stopped totally by the end of the season.

Lifestyle management

I'll make sure I get 8 hours' sleep every night before a match night, starting from match 1 of the pre-season tour.

After every training session, I'll make sure that I get into the habit of refuelling and rehydrating within an hour. Begin this straight away.

Focus on the PROCESS... and the OUTCOME will take care of itself

Total COMMITMENT TO THE PROCESS... ONE DAY AT A TIME

CRITICAL TARGETS	Name: Date:
The SMARTA System **Set – Do – Review**	
Skills and tactics training • • • •	
Fitness training and physical preparation… • • • •	
'Training the brain' – attitude and mental skills • • • •	
Lifestyle management • • • •	
Focus on the PROCESS . . . and the OUTCOME will take care of itself **Total COMMITMENT TO THE PROCESS… ONE DAY AT A TIME**	

BUILDING ON THE TIME-ELEMENT OF GOAL SETTING.

It's useful to check how your goals mesh together to help maintain motivation over time. It's all very well starting off with high motivation for the first few days of improvement, but the trick is to keep the motivation for change going from week to week, month to month and through a whole season. That's why it's important that you get a sense of maintaining change over a much longer period of time. You need to make sure that with goal-setting there are some *long-term* goals well in

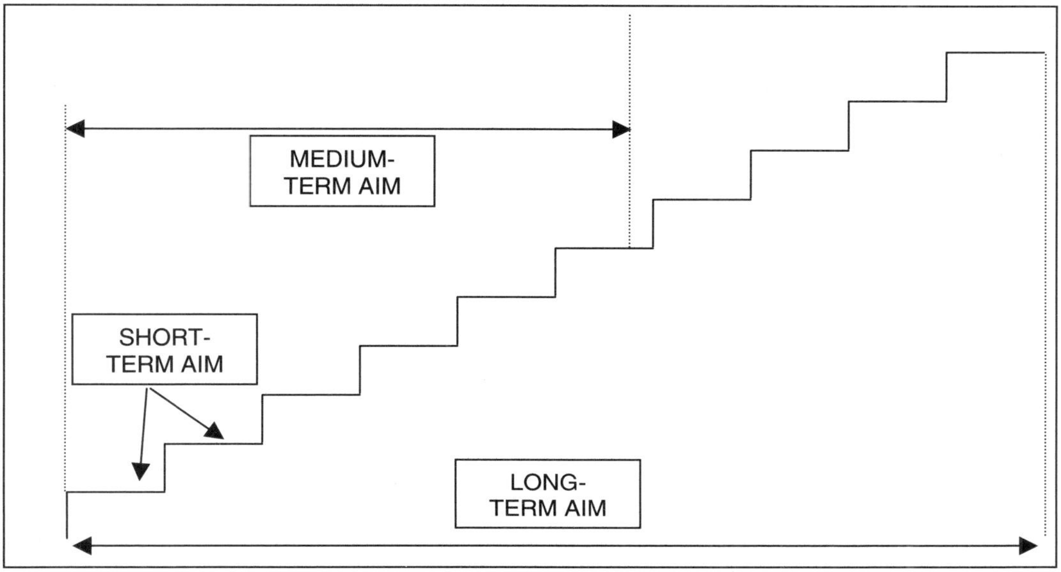

the distance, and between where you are today, and that point in time, there are some *medium-term* targets and then *short-term* targets for the next couple of weeks. Using the idea of a staircase really helps with this, and allows you to get a real sense that something that is being focused upon today will ultimately impact upon your success in the long term. If you go up the staircase one step at a time, and achieve each step as effectively as possible, then by default you'll get closer to your main aim. Therefore, you can focus on the process of improving today, knowing that your success today will impact upon success in the future. Try to plan out your goal-setting pathway so that there is a short, medium and long-term structure to the whole venture. If it helps, think about developing daily goal habits that help you achieve weekly improvements that, in turn, accumulate to achieve monthly targets.

With a good time-frame laid out, and medium-term target check points put in place, you can make sure that there is adaptability within your goal-setting timetable. So, if progress is quicker than expected, you can bring the targets forward in time. However, if for some reason you are unable to make the progress you would like (injury, illness, change of club, and so on) then you can slightly amend the whole programme of progress. So, don't be afraid to adapt the timetable if you need to! Flexibility in goal-setting is vital.

Goals Over Time

- Daily Goals . . .
- Weekly Goals . . .
- Monthly Goals . . .

What are you doing today that will take you one step closer to your main goal?

How many steps did you take last week towards your main goal?

GOALS ARE NOT ALL OR NOTHING!

We find that in sport, goal-setting tends to bring out the perfectionist in people. Although it's great to have the drive and dedication that perfectionism brings, it's also important to make sure that it doesn't stop you learning from your goals. Perfectionistic thinking and goal-setting tends to go like this . . . 'Well . . . it wasn't totally successful, therefore I failed.' With an attempt to achieve a target being defined as failure, chances are that you will not now review the attempt thoroughly because of thinking, 'What on earth could I learn from a failure?'

To avoid this happening we always encourage players to think in the following ways:

1. Set multiple levels of goals to help you identify your degree of success.
2. If you don't do 1, always use 0–100 per cent success ratings when evaluating goals.

Goal-Setting Levels

My dream result for this goal is . . .

My realistic result for this goal is . . .

The minimum level of achievement I will accept from myself is . . .

Multiple Levels of Goals

When setting goals, try to make sure that you consider what would constitute:

A. Dream Result

B. Realistic Result

C. Minimum Acceptable Result

The dream result refers to everything going as well as possible, having a dream day with everything falling into place to allow a great level to be achieved. The realistic result refers to a level of performance that you know will be very satisfactory, is achievable if all goes well, and would mark some good success. The minimum acceptable result refers to the level of performance that you are unwilling to drop below. Anything lower than this and you would feel you have not done yourself justice.

Within these three levels, draw upon positive and negative motivation, and really provide a good framework within which to evaluate your goals. So, once the goals have been set, you can't change the goal-posts and you have to stick to the different levels once you have performed.

> Dreams I reckon, constitute roughly 75% of the make-up of any true football man.
>
> **Ron Atkinson**
>
> (In Pickering's *Great Sporting Quotations*, 2000)

The Success Scale

For each goal, I know I will be anywhere between 0 and 100% successful.

Make sure I focus on getting as high up the scale as possible. What does each percentage mean for me?

◆——————————◆

0% 50% 100%

Success Ratings

If you don't want to set the different levels of goals, then you must make sure that any goal you set is always going to be evaluated on a 0-100 per cent success scale. Therefore, you can be 5 per cent successful or 100 per cent successful. You are of course trying to get as high up the success scale as possible each time you attempt a goal, but you have to recognize that not every attempt will be 100% successful. Make sure you don't lose valuable learning information and motivation by ignoring your level of success.

Therefore, when you set your goals, you should have a clear idea of what the different levels of success would actually mean for you. So, what would equate to 50 per cent success, 75 per cent success, and so on. If you decide this in advance, you then need to make sure that you stick to these levels when it comes to evaluation in the final step. This is easier said than done, so make sure you are hard on yourself, and make sure you don't change the goalposts!

When setting goals, it's always important to check through our goal-setting rules to make sure that the features listed in the box on the right are present.

✔ **S**pecific – You've really nailed down the goals and there is no ambiguity in what you are trying to achieve, and how you will know whether you have been successful or not. You should not have to ask the question 'What do you mean by that?' when talking about the goals set.

✔ **M**otivational– if goals are going to be effective then they have to give players a buzz . . . they have to want to achieve that goal. If goals light the touch paper of motivation, then quality of work and commitment will follow.

✔ **A**ssessable – There's no point setting a goal if you don't work out how you're going to know whether it's been achieved or not. Whether using game statistics, or 1 to 10 rating scales, you have to assess the goal in order to work out where to go next.

✔ **R**ealistic – Goals have to move players out of their comfort zones, but they have to be within the realms of possibility. Too easy, and the goals have little impact, too hard and they'll reduce confidence over time. You'll be able to use our levels of goal-setting to help with this.

✔ **T**ime-phased – make sure you build in some time elements to your goal-setting. Goals without deadlines or evaluation points lose their impact, so always make sure you build up the short, medium and long-term dates when the goals will be assessed.

✔ **A**ccountability – players must buy into the goals that have been set, and accept that they will be accountable for their part in achieving the goals. Always make sure coaches and players know and accept what their responsibilities are in the goal-setting process.

PHASE 2 – DO

Phase Two is very straightforward. You have now to put your goals into action. As much as possible you have got to do the things that will mean you train or perform totally focused on the intention of making the goals become reality. The goals you have set should give you direction and focus for the session or match. You should have clear things to concentrate on, and specific reference points to keep coming back to in order to ensure that you are staying true to the factors that you know will make a difference. The goals you have set will allow you to make use of the cue cards and pre-performance planners that we'll introduce in Step 7.

The goals have created your agenda for training or playing, and the key challenge we'd throw out to you is to see how good you can actually get at turning your goals into actions. Many people are good at setting goals, but few are really world class at ensuring that these goals actually turn into actions every time.

If you know that whenever you set a goal, 100 per cent of the time you will follow this through exactly, you will be taking a huge step towards developing a world-class performance mindset. Imagine beginning a match, *knowing* you will definitely put your goals into action. If you then know that you are great at setting goals that will produce a great performance you cannot be anything other than full of true confidence – you know you're going to play well!

So, see how good you can be at putting goals into action.

The Learning Cycle 4 Steps to Successful Reviewing

1. **Experience** – The key rule here is to make sure that you have immersed yourself 100 per cent into your goals for the game. The closer you come to doing everything that you said you were going to do, the more you can now learn. If you said you were going to do something and then didn't, all you can really learn from that is that you don't stick with your plans!

2. **Reflection** – When looking back on your goals, you have to simply try and record what you did or didn't do. Don't get into any judgements of good or bad at this point – just get down matter of fact detail of what you did compared to what you said you were going to do. Try to imagine you are making notes for someone else – this will help make sure that you don't let emotion get in the way of good reviewing!

3. **Appraisal** – Having worked out how well you did what you said you were going to do, you can now start to work out how and why you got to the levels of goal achievement that you did. You need to know *why*; if you did really well, you need to know how to repeat it, and if you didn't do well, you need to know what to avoid in the future.

4. **Planning** – Armed with the knowledge from 2 and 3, you can now set out some clear targets and aims in order to build on the knowledge you have gained.

PHASE 3 – REVIEW

We cover reviewing performances later in the book, as it's important to consider this process in its own right. However, not enough is made of reviewing goals in most books we read. In reality, this is the most important part of the whole process, because if you don't review, how can you learn what worked and what didn't? How can you plan for executing the goal the same or better next time around? You need to see that the three parts, Set – Do – Review, have equal importance in the process of developing as a player. You might look to spend at least double the time reviewing the goals as you did setting them. If you are going to get the next goals set at the right level to maximize motivation, learning and confidence, then you need to give yourself time to appraise your efforts.

Within business settings people often refer to Kolb's learning cycle as a way for developing knowledge, and in terms of reviewing your goals, we'd recommend that you take a few simple ideas from this approach and apply it to your reviewing to make sure that you are becoming highly successful in your ability to review, as well as aiming to be the best that you can be on the pitch. There's nothing spectacular about the ideas behind this cycle, and the main rule is to ensure that you adhere to the process, and keep using it to make sure you are getting the most information out of every Step – Do – Review cycle you go through. It's easy to skip the reviewing in football, because as soon as one training session is over, or one match is finished, the focus changes instantly to the next challenge. However, in order to keep your momentum going, and get the most out of the goals you're setting, you have to really focus on the fact that a match or session is not over until you have reviewed it and learned from it. The ref's whistle blowing is not the end of the match in relation to your psychological development!

You can use the reviewing questions that we've provided next to help you make sure that you have the right starting points to your review process.

Review Questions.

1. How well did I do what I said I was going to do? Did I put the goals into action?
2. How successfully did I achieve my goals? 0 – 100 per cent?
3. What worked well in helping me towards my goals?
4. What did not work so well and detracted from my level of success?
5. What main reason/s would I give for the result I achieved?
6. What changes should I make to the goals I set based on this result?
7. How well will I make sure I get the same or better level of success with the next goal?

You should make sure that you look at goal-setting as a skill, and from now on, see how proficient you can become at setting, doing and reviewing your goals. We guarantee that if you enhance your goal-setting skills, there will be an accompanying improvement in your consistency in those areas that you have focused your goals onto.

STEP 2

It's a Game of Confidence: The Positive Thinking Plan

> **Cantona on Confidence**
>
> I've said in the past that I could play single-handedly against eleven players and win. I believe in myself. Sometimes it's crazy, I know. Give me a bicycle and I believe that I can beat Chris Boardman's one-hour record. If someone says to me, 'Get on this bicycle and beat the world record,' I say: 'OK. I've got a chance.' It is that belief which drives me on. No matter what the situation, I always think I have a chance of winning.
>
> Victory is all-important, and to succeed you have to believe.
>
> There is a place for doubt: doubt makes you question yourself, it makes you want to win. Doubt leads to fear, and fear is what fuels every great challenge. But the trick is to transcend that fear, to believe in your own abilities so that the team can win. I've always had that quality. Even if it's crazy, it's part of who I am. There's something inside me that always believes I can do it.
>
> **Eric Cantona**
>
> (*Cantona on Cantona*, 1996)

STATING THE OBVIOUS

Did you know that the more confident a player or a team is, then the better they will perform? And if they are not confident, then they generally won't play well? This mind-blowingly obvious relationship between confidence and performance is one that is seldom taken advantage of because of the perception that confidence is a mystical commodity that comes and goes as it pleases, that 'can't be bought', and that as we can't see it, we can't take control of it. This section will show you that confidence can be earned, and can be controlled, if it is built in the correct way, and then maintained appropriately. You and your team have choices with confidence – you can choose to take control of it and make the approaches discussed become part and parcel of your daily/weekly training programme, or you can choose to carry on believing that confidence is out of your control, and that you'll get it only by getting a win, because after all, in football, one of the most frequently used quotes is 'All we need is a win to get our confidence back'. This approach simply perpetuates the myth that confidence is all about results, and totally sets up a player or team for massive confidence peaks and troughs throughout a season – not an approach we would recommend.

Confidence is possibly the most important psychological commodity within sport. From amateur player to international performer,

> One of my weaknesses as a footballer was a shortage of self-belief. **If I had had more self-confidence, I would have been a better player**, and maybe a better manager as well. Confidence, or rather the lack of it, was still an issue even when I felt well-established at Liverpool. It's the way I am, a chink in my armoury. I wish I had more belief in my own ability. Maybe I have too much respect for other people; although people I respected made me captain of Celtic and Liverpool, and also Scotland, but I still lacked self-belief. **I could have done better for club and country, if I'd had more confidence**.
>
> **Kenny Dalglish**
> (*Dalglish: My Autobiography*, 1996)

more often than not, sport psychologists will at some point focus their work on helping improve confidence. We have stopped being surprised at how frequently we get requests to help improve confidence, as more often than not, players don't take the time to train their confidence in the first place, so without a strong confidence foundation, it is not surprising that the level of belief you have in yourself slips very quickly. We've already outlined the importance of robust self-confidence and self-belief in making the difference in the introductory section. This Step will give you the knowledge of how to give your players the best chance of getting hold of, and keeping, these winning mind factors.

Our aim in this chapter is to give you an insight into the confidence challenge for players and teams, with a view to outlining just why it is so important to put solid confidence foundations in place prior to getting a crisis in confidence. We will then introduce the simple techniques that should be carried out as a matter of course with all players in order to *build* a solid confidence platform. Having considered these 'non-negotiables', we'll then focus on the kind of common sense 'maintenance' activities that need to be put in place to keep the level of confidence as consistent as possible. More than any area in sport psychology, confidence truly outlines how important it is to think of your mind as you think of your fitness . . . you don't wait to get unfit before you start to train fitness of the body . . . therefore, don't wait to lose confidence before you start to work on making it strong!

We should also point out that our ideas in this chapter are very much focused on getting players and teams to build the *robust* confidence that we introduced in the introductory section. Rather than super-high confidence, we believe that you are better off building confidence that very firmly stays in place. Contrast this approach to aiming to inflate confidence to a really high level, but ending up with belief that is easily undermined at the first sign of a negative situation or outcome. As with any structure, if you get the foundation elements strong, then the overall strength and resistance is far greater. Skimp on the foundations, and the structure is quickly undermined, resulting in having to build all over again. Eric Cantona's opening quote to this section perfectly illustrates that once confidence is built really well, it can actually become a personal quality that is a feature of everything you do.

> In my view confidence is half of the game.
>
> **Kevin Keegan** speaking on BBC's *Football Focus*

> Self-belief is such an important element in football.
>
> **David Beckham**
> (*David Beckham: My Side*, 2003)

BUT WHAT IS CONFIDENCE?

Simply put, confidence is your level of belief that you can achieve something. The 'something' element of the definition is really important to helping understand confidence losses and confidence gains. Strikers often talk about losing confidence in front of goal. In this case, they are probably saying that they have lost confidence in the outcome of scoring. This could be as a result of coming up against defenders and goalkeepers who are playing well, and thus making finishing more difficult than normal. It might be as a result of poor service in the box, so clear chances are not made and the striker has been faced with rushed, pressurized chances that are less likely to be converted. Equally, the lack of goals might result from poor decision-making by the striker, and thinking too much, thus giving the player 'paralysis by analysis'. Some of these reasons are within the striker's control, and they can do something about changing performance. However, some of the reasons are not within the player's control, so they have to work hard to make sure these uncontrollable factors are not being allowed to dent confidence in them and their ability.

Whatever the reasons, the lack of positive feedback from seeing the ball in the back of the net has started to make the player experience some sort of doubt. However, confidence is influenced by much more than just results, and making sure that confidence is anchored in ability rather than results is critical. On questioning strikers, it is likely that they would still believe they have a certain level of heading ability. Equally, they would still believe in their ability to strike with either foot inside 12 yards. Their ability to make good runs off defenders would probably remain stable, and their ability to take defenders on and put them under pressure in the box would be consistent. Therefore, the player has not lost the confidence that they have the equipment to score the goals – they have stopped focusing on how to score, and are thinking about the outcome before they have given themselves a chance to go through the process of having an attempt on goal. So, in this situation, the player has to work hard on making sure that their confidence is based upon the skills and abilities that they know provide them with the chance of scoring goals. As with the goal-setting previously, they have to focus on the *process* of scoring goals, rather than the *outcome* of scoring goals. The confidence needs to be based upon the ability to carry out the process, rather than relying solely upon getting the results.

So, it's clear that there are different layers to a player's, or a team's, confidence, and your ability to decide which layer is in need of attention to help with confidence is critical to how effectively you help build and maintain confidence. Eric Cantona's quote at the beginning of this section helps to outline the layers. It is very clear Cantona has great confidence in

> *When managers need to develop confidence in the team, they cannot rely exclusively on beliefs such as this . . .*
>
> The most important thing in football to breed confidence is to win games and unfortunately that just hasn't happened recently.
>
> **Eddie Gray**
> (itv/football.com, 2003)

Are You Really a Confident Player?

1. Confidence in myself as a person.
2. Confidence in my abilities as a player.
3. Confidence in my ability to make effective use of my abilities *every time I need to.*

How would you rate yourself on each of these out of 100?

himself as a person, and he clearly states the importance in having belief in your abilities. So we need to pick out confidence in you the person, and confidence in your specific sporting abilities. Finally, there is the confidence in your ability to win, or get the results you are striving for, which really means your confidence to put your abilities into effective use – you have the ammunition and you know how to use it. Surprisingly, many players *know* they have the ability, but they are not confident in *how* to use the abilities in order to produce a performance when they need to.

Real confidence losses come when teams or individuals repeatedly play badly, and don't get results – the evidence is showing that their ability is disappearing, rather than being temporarily lost! All layers of confidence are being undermined, so something radical has to be done in order to turn this situation around.

Something you also need to consider when we're talking about confidence, is the obvious question of 'confidence in what?' We often hear players and managers saying things like, 'I've just lost confidence' or 'All we need is to get our confidence back again.' If these statements are to be of any use, then there needs to be a clear understanding of what exactly is the reason for the lost confidence.

The performance profile we introduced in Phase 1 can really help with understanding where the confidence is breaking down with individual players, and obviously, if you are using the profiling with a team, it can help establish loss of collective confidence too. As performance has been broken down into specific parts, and then rated in relation to the levels that you aspire to, you can quickly begin to determine which elements of performance are being identified as weak, and therefore, undermining confidence.

The use of the performance profile to aid with confidence highlights the influential role that goal-setting and goal-reviewing can have on confidence. The very obvious relationship between goal-setting and confidence is that if you set a goal and achieve it, you effectively give yourself positive feedback from the achievement, and increase your belief that you'll be able to successfully achieve the same, or similar goal next time you set the target. So, if we've got many small goals focused upon improving and achieving in relation to specific parts of the performance profile, this means that we have many small possibilities of injecting confidence into our system.

THE CONFIDENCE CHALLENGE IN FOOTBALL

When thinking about building and maintaining confidence, it's important to consider why we need to think so much about helping players take control of their self-belief. Have a look at the pie chart below. In relation to the normal player, we can assume that the white portion of the pie (75 per cent) relates to those things that are working well for a player, and are consistently good about their game. The grey portion (20 per cent) might be the elements of their game that are not as good as they could be, and need to be worked on in training. Finally, the black portion (5 per cent) represents those areas of their game that actually cause problems, bring about mistakes, and are weaknesses that the opposition would look to exploit. If our player is going to improve, then they need to address the weaker areas,

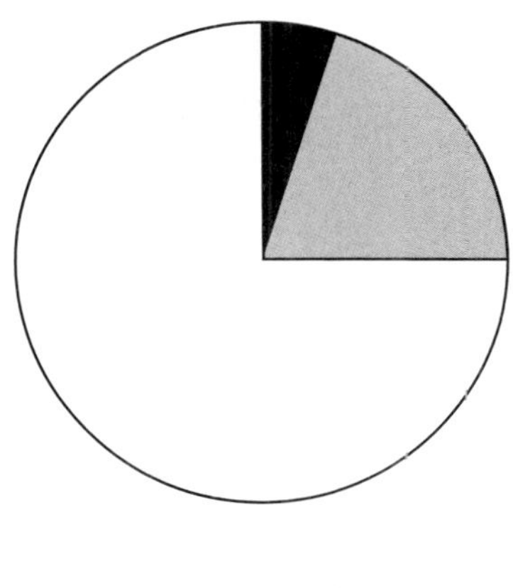

> When Brian Clough first came into Nottingham Forest, everyone at that time picked on all the things that I couldn't do, as far as football was concerned – I couldn't tackle, I couldn't head, I wasn't the quickest person – but it didn't seem to worry him at all and he concentrated on things that I was good at.
>
> **John Robertson**
> (In Bolchover & Brady, *The 90 Minute Manager*, 2002)

and work on improving the whole picture. So, we have a player who is primarily made up of positive qualities, but has some areas of performance to work on – no surprises there. However, we now need to focus on how much time the player actually spends thinking about each of these areas, and how this changes the way they see themselves as a player.

In order to strengthen the weaker areas, the player is repeatedly told that they are not up to standard on key areas, and that they must work on improving these areas of their game. Therefore, it is possible that the majority of the player's training time is spent thinking about the things they are not doing well enough, and the things they are not good enough at. They will be comparing themselves to the players who are good at all of the things they are weak at, and seeing that they are not up to scratch. This is the extreme end of the continuum, but simply put, the more time we spend focused on what we don't do right, the more chance we have of losing confidence. The impact of the negative thinking time is made all the greater if the player has not taken the time to reflect upon the areas of their game that should be giving them confidence. Equally, consider how much positive feedback players are given in relation to negative feedback. We're quick to identify problems, and let someone know about them, but we're usually slow to sit a player down and systematically give them positive feedback to help them build a strong base to their confidence. More often than not, players won't take the time to build their confidence for themselves, so we have to consider how we're making sure that 'confidence building' is actually part and parcel of their training.

Another analogy that we have seen used very effectively to help highlight the confidence challenge is the 'confidence cup'. Our strengths and abilities fill the cup up to the top. However, the things that we do not do well, and undermine our confidence, drill holes in the cup, making our confidence drain away. Some holes are really big, the major

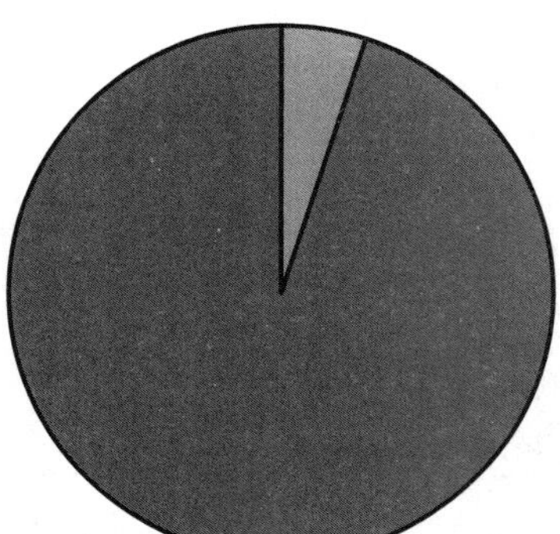

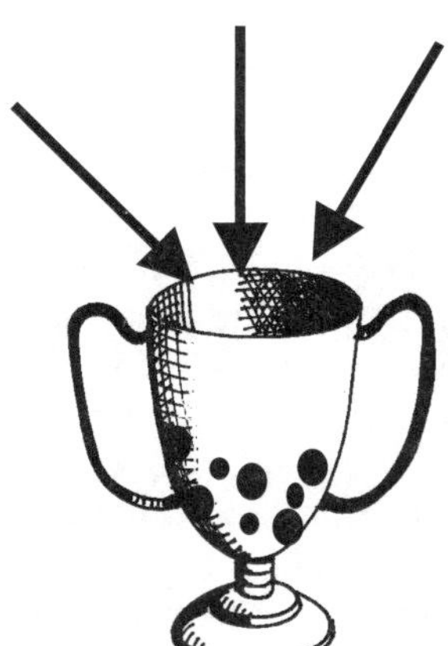

The confidence cup.

> When two teams are equally strong in technique, tactics and feel for the game, the team with the greater confidence is going to win.
>
> **Sven-Goran Eriksson**
> (*Sven-Goran Eriksson on Football*, 2002)

weaknesses, and some are small. The small holes slowly undermine the confidence over time, whereas the larger holes are a constant, nagging doubt that is not dealt with. If we don't keep making sure we top the confidence up (as well as trying to permanently fill the holes by eradicating the weaknesses), then we are left with very little confidence to draw upon.

The challenge is very obvious when spelled out like this. Of course, we have to be aware of weaknesses and things to work on that will improve performance, and we're not suggesting being positive for the sake of being positive, or ignoring weaknesses. But, it is usually the case that time is not spent on developing a strong background of confidence, that equips the players to address their weaknesses, safe in the knowledge that they still have many positive qualities to offer. At worst, we need to make sure that players are working on getting a balance between their knowledge of the things that give them confidence, and a focus upon doing something to improve weak areas.

Team Confidence

Building individual confidence becomes even more important when you think about spreading belief and confidence through your team. It's clear to see that the most successful teams are also the most confident ones . . . and this confidence has not always come simply from winning. The confidence has been developed even before victories have been achieved. From all of the successful teams we've worked with and studied, there are some simple, but clear similarities between the confidence of these teams. We'll build more on this in **Step 6**, as it's an essential element of strong team psychology. However, we need to introduce the ideas here to really highlight just how important it is to make sure that building confidence in individual players becomes part and parcel of your whole approach to psychology. The confidence of these teams is best described with our simple diagram overleaf.

Team confidence is a key factor in success on the big day.
© EMPICS

First, each player in the high-performing teams has really strong confidence in themselves. They know they can do their job really well, and believe they're the best player for the position or role in question. Second, all of the players can look around the changing room and training ground and see that they are surrounded by players in whom they have confidence – they believe their team-mates can carry out their roles effectively, so there is no need to worry about covering for a weak link, or doubt the decisions and actions of the other players. This confidence in others now results in each individual player being able to concentrate 100 per cent on their own game. The final part of the jigsaw can now be put in place – confidence in the team as a collective unit. When the players think about the team playing together, they are confident in the team as a whole. Therefore, not only is there confidence in the individual elements of the team, there is also confidence in how these blend together, execute tactics and combat the opposition – *as a unit*. In this case, 1 + 2 really does equal 3!

> The ability to make the right decision – and then dare to do the right thing in all situations – is decisive at the top of the modern game. If one player isn't up for it mentally, the whole team collapses.
>
> **Sven-Goran Eriksson**
> (*Sven-Goran Eriksson on Football*, 2002)

The most important thing about this simple model is that if any player lacks confidence in themselves, then there is very little chance that the other two elements of confidence will exist. So if you're going to get a truly confident team, then you're going to have to make sure that each of your players has solid individual confidence. The key to team success is individual belief . . . so make sure you get this building block in place.

So, when you look at your team, start thinking about how you would rate confidence levels in each of the three areas. On average, how confident are your players in themselves? How confident are they in each

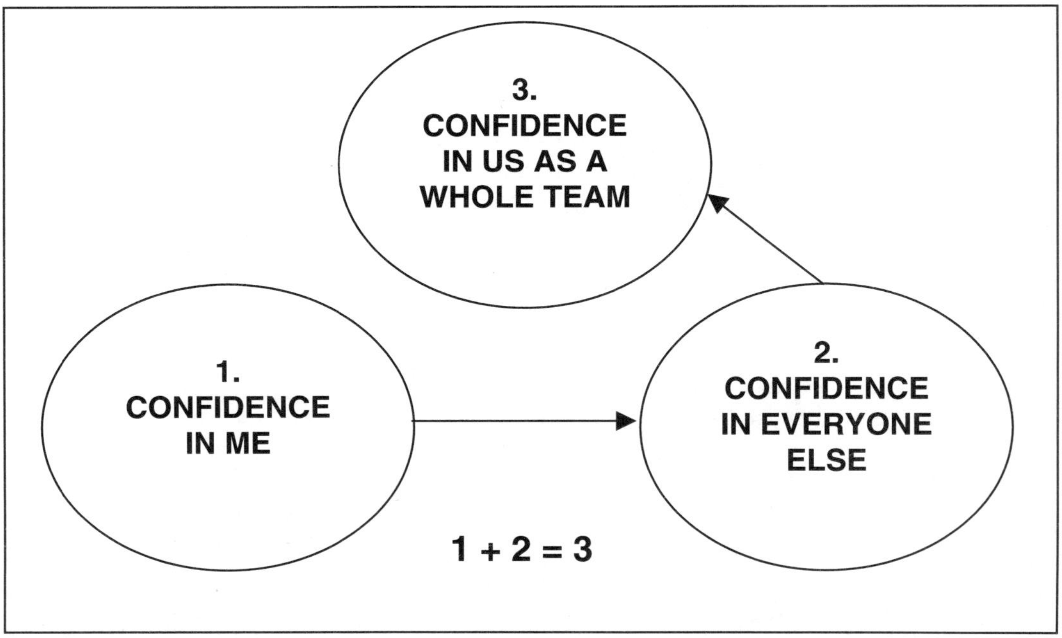

other, and how much confidence do the players have in the team as a unit. Once you can get a feel for how each element is working, you can start to think about how you might use some of the ideas in this section and in Step 7 to help improve your confidence levels.

BUILDING STRONG CONFIDENCE FOUNDATIONS

The next sections are going to focus on the most regularly used and most simply developed confidence-building strategies. Once these strategies have started to be employed, then it is possible to start using training and matches to ensure that confidence is maintained. We would recommend that all players are encouraged to get their strong foundations in place by making sure they carry out at least one of these confidence-building techniques. The trick is to find the one that suits you, as not all players will respond the same way to a specific approach.

Self-Talk – Being Your Own Supporter!

What players say to themselves is one of the most simple and important ways of ensuring confidence is being built and maintained. *Self-talk* is a huge influence on the strength and level of our confidence. If a player repeatedly engages in positive self-talk, where the language used is focused on strengths, positive contributions to the team, positive self-image, and positive expectations of future individual performances, then they are very obviously going to feel more confident and be more likely to perform well. Equally, if a player repeatedly engages in negative self-talk, where they focus on weaknesses, mistakes, and doubts about future performances, then of course, performance and confidence suffer. As we stress throughout this book, nobody tells us what to think, so we make choices about what we say to ourselves and what we focus upon. Therefore, if we are going to *choose* the right content for our self-talk, we have to put in some groundwork so that we know the key things to say to ourselves to build personal confidence. Once we know the content of the self-talk, then we have to challenge ourselves to see how effectively we can keep using it.

We'll focus specifically on the detail of self-talk a little later and you'll see how important it is to be aware of how you talk to yourself, as well as what you say. But first, we need to identify those things that we can say to ourselves that will be really useful in building a sound base to confidence.

Choosing Your Personal Chants!

Self-affirmations, or reminders, are a set of specifically selected self-statements that focus a player on positive abilities and skills. The statements can also focus the player on previous training and preparation factors that are central to confidence, as well as match performances. Through the use of reminder statements the player immerses in the conscious mind these positive thoughts that are associated with the why and the how of performing at their best. Repeated use of the positive statements causes them to be planted in the subconscious, and therefore makes sure that the deeply held beliefs of our ability and skills are constantly influenced by this positive perspective. These enhanced beliefs increase confidence before and during competition and ultimately performance is likely to be more consistently of a high level.

The reminders are almost like having a 'rent-a-crowd' who are permanently with you, chanting really positive things about you, your game, and your achievements. If we had a crowd constantly reminding us of these positive elements and experiences, it is very likely that we would soon end up with a very positive view of ourselves. The important thing about these positive statements is that they are accurate and believable. These reminders are

> Aggression is based on insecurity. Real fighting spirit is based on inner security and self-confidence.
>
> **Sven-Goran Eriksson**
> (*Sven-Goran Eriksson on Football*, 2002)

not simply being positive for the sake of being positive – we have to know that the statements are truthful and meaningful if they are to gain a firm place in our subconscious.

Sometimes players think this idea is too obvious to be effective. Our response is usually along the lines of . . . 'OK, well, let's select a list of negative statements to repeat to yourself instead for the next month, and we'll see how you get on.' This approach is very obvious, but it is also obvious that players don't carry out this kind of positive self-coaching, so they are not making sure they have taken steps to make confidence as *solid* as possible. If it is obvious how powerful the negative approach would be, then the professional thing to do is make sure that the positive reminders are used to ensure that confident thoughts become part and parcel of weekly preparation for matches. We also know that given the choice, when left to their own devices, humans will carry out negative thinking, and focus on doubts. Given that we'll revert to negative thinking, we need to ensure that we are making very deliberate attempts to counteract this!

You can see on the next chart that we have provided some examples of the positive reminders players have used in the past. We'd normally recommend a list of four to eight statements that relate to the positive elements of performance, and of course, these can be updated as often as is necessary to ensure that past and present positives are being used to underpin confidence.

Once these reminders have been identified, they can be written on a card and read daily. Eventually the statements seem easier to repeat with conviction, and the player becomes more comfortable with the whole process of positive thinking. They are then able to begin using the statements during training and in the lead-up to matches, and they become part and parcel of the confidence building and maintenance process for the player. The aim is to get the player in a position where their natural inclination is to think positively, rather than doubting their ability. They are focused on exploiting the strengths they are aware of, rather than playing to avoid weaknesses being exposed. If it helps, some players might like to get the positive statements recorded onto a CD or DVD, and then play it in the car or bus when they are on their own on the way to training, or perhaps prior to going to sleep.

General Reminders

My training quality is always high.

I know I always rise to the challenge on match day.

I am improving my all-round game each season.

My ability to read the game never lets me down.

I'm stronger and quicker than any player in my position that I know.

Every manager I've played for has told me they know that they can rely on me under pressure.

My fitness is never in doubt.

I'm always 100 per cent committed in a tackle.

Developing personalized lists

1. By looking at a Performance Profile (Step 1), or through reflecting back over previous seasons, write down short sentences that effectively describe your repeated positive

My General Reminder Chart

•

•

•

•

qualities. Think about positive things that team-mates, coaches, or press reports have *consistently* said about you over previous seasons. If it helps, aim to have at least one statement that refers to skill, one that refers to fitness, one that refers to mindset or attitude, and one that refers to how you play in match situations. Write these down in the chart provided.

2. Put the chart in a place where you will be able to see it every day, and make sure you read the statements to yourself at least once a day. As you read, actually say the words to yourself (either in your head or out loud).
3. When you feel comfortable repeating the statements to yourself, try using them prior to training, and then try using them in the build-up to a match.
4. Periodically check to see if you need to add new statements. This will keep the content up to date and meaningful, and you won't be tempted to stop using the affirmations because they are so old and have become meaningless to you.
5. Keep doing your positive reminders training even when you're feeling positive

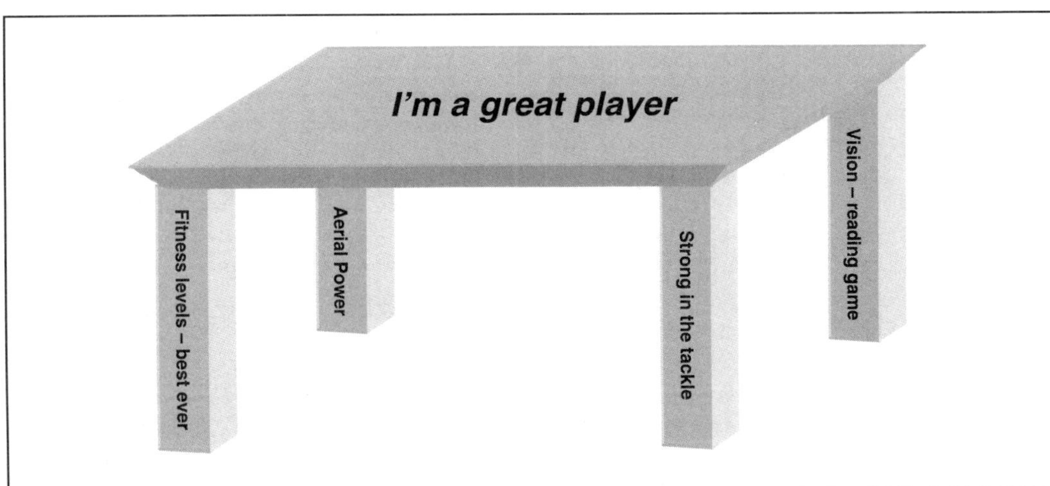

and things are going well. This is the most important time to keep the positivity going.

If it helps, you might want to think of these positive reminders as a table. The table top can refer to a specific performance statement, or your overall ability as a player, and then each of the legs of the table is a positive reminder that is focused on your strengths and is therefore a 'support' to the table top. The more legs you have, the more solid the table will be and the evidence backs up why you are going to be able to produce a performance. Even with three legs the table will stand up, but the more legs you put under the table top, the more the table will hold firm in different situations, conditions, against different opposition. We've found this approach works really well for the kind of players who need to 'see' how things are building up, so why not try it out for yourself and build your own table to remind you why you should be positive about the way you play.

PERSONAL PERFORMANCE HIGHLIGHTS

Another effective self-talk approach that can be a good specific source of confidence is the development of specific statements that remind the player of specific personal achievements or great performances. Carrying this process out ensures that the player takes the time to dwell on the career highlights and focus on how such highs can be repeated in the future. This list can focus upon great personal performances that were very satisfying, even though the team did not actually get a win. Of course, a great performance and a team win are usually the most important, but it is important not to throw away confidence influencing performances due to a poor result.

You can see on the next chart some examples of the kind of specific ideas we are talking about for these specific reminders. It's possible for everyone, whatever their level, to write down these specific pointers, but we have also used the same idea to help create video highlight films. It's exactly the same idea, but the player gets to relive highlights and get all the positive benefits through video that can be achieved through replaying the experiences in their mind.

When compiling your lists of reminders, make sure you are not modest. These lists are for personal use, so nobody else needs to see them. With these lists, there is no place for worrying about being big-headed or arrogant. These lists are accurate, factual, and if a player is truly going to believe in themselves then there has to be a certain amount of personal trumpet blowing! You have to take the plunge

Personal Achievement Reminders

When I made my club debut, I was the youngest ever player selected for the first team.

I was consistently our most influential player in the last five games of last season.

I have the best clean sheets record of any keeper at the club over the last ten years.

I got four Player of the Match awards in my first season.

My defensive performance last year against Westchester United in the bad conditions was by far the best of the season.

I am the club's quickest ever player to fifty goals.

My pass to set-up the winning goal in the cup final was superb skill under pressure.

into the confidence deep-end if this approach is really going to work. For players with low confidence, this process of becoming confident and comfortable with the positivity will take more time, so be patient!

The personal achievement reminders are usually most helpful when there has been a run of below par performances, or confidence is on the wane. Holding this list back to be used when needed can often mean it has more impact.

You can use the blank chart to record your specific personal achievement reminders, and once again, make sure you reflect on your career to date to ensure that you really get the best possible factors included in your reminder list.

My Personal Achievement Reminder Chart

-
-
-
-

As with the general reminders list, personal achievement reminders should be updated regularly, with new items being added, or old ones replaced. Another additional idea that can help with making confidence more robust is to extend the list to other aspects of life. In order to feel confident in sport, it's usually necessary to feel confident in yourself generally. Identifying achievements in education, business or with family can be really useful. Indeed, acknowledging successes relating to social and family life can be an effective way of boosting overall self-esteem that can then translate into confidence for performance. So, it's worth considering life as a whole and drawing as many positives as possible from different areas. They will all contribute to the creation of that ideal match mindset.

LOOKING TO THE FUTURE – MATCH SPECIFIC REMINDERS

The two previous sets of reminders have been focused on helping to create a foundation of confidence based on things that are already in place, and previous achievements. However, the challenge with sport is making sure that this confidence can be carried into the future, into the matches to come. Therefore, once the player is happy with using positive thinking, it is possible to develop statements that can be instrumental in developing a positive mindset for a specific match or opponent. We've found this helpful with players who like to give themselves a set of positive reminders to focus on just before, and even during the match.

If you think this technique may be useful for you, why not write out several statements on the chart provided in the week leading up to your next match? Read the card each time you add another statement, and keep focused on the positive statements that are helping you shape *how* you are intending to play, and the

Match Specific Positive Statements

Stay positive in my body language from minute 1 to minute 90.

Be positive like Renaldo every time I'm within twenty yards of goal.

My aerial strength will be a big advantage for us.

Be strong and quick in my communication to the back four.

Whatever the score, I will stay positive and look to take the game to them.

Start as I mean to go on – I will dominate my opponent.

My great form in training is going to be taken into the match.

Stay positive, stay strong, keep backing yourself.

My Match Preparation Chart

-
-
-
-

attitudes you will take into the game. Obviously, the card can go in your kit bag and you can read it through in the locker room as an element of your final mental preparation.

Whatever the team you are playing for, and whoever the opponent, this approach can really keep you focused on how you are going to make sure *your strengths* and your *essential attitudes* will feature in the match. Having read the statements in the lead-up to the game, it is then much more likely that under the pressure of the game you'll bring the most helpful thoughts to the forefront of your mind, so you stay focused on the recipe that is most likely to bring you a successful performance.

It's Good to Talk . . . to Yourself!

As you can see from the content of the various reminders, a lot can be achieved by deliberately talking to yourself in a certain way . . . choosing the content of your self-talk. Although we recommend finding some time to practise using the reminders, there is also a lot of benefit to be gained from becoming aware of the general way in which you talk to yourself, and be aware of when some of this talk might be negatively focused. This is easier said than done, but we'll give you some ideas here of what to be on the look-out for, and how to make the ongoing efforts to keep the self-talk as helpful as possible. Using self-talk effectively is a critical component in both building and maintaining confidence.

The key to successful reframing is twofold. First, don't try to deny or ignore that there is

> I don't know how many times I've gone off to be by myself at a World Championships or an Olympic Games with the minutes ticking down ever so slowly, with thousands of thoughts in my mind. 'What the f*** am I doing here? Why am I doing it? I don't want to be here. It's absolutely horrible.' At Atlanta I was just walking around saying to myself: 'The pressure's too much. I just can't do this at all.' If somebody had given me any sort of excuse at all to pull out, I'd have happily done so. But then you have to mentally give yourself a slap and say, 'Steve, if you keep thinking like this you're not going to get the best out of yourself. You're not going to win.'
>
> **Sir Steve Redgrave**
>
> (*A Golden Age: The Autobiography*, 2000)

some degree of concern or negativity in your mind. Denial will stop you taking positive action to controlling the self-talk. Recognize that your mind is posing some doubt in order to get you to provide a clear set of solutions about *how* you are going to handle things using your set of strengths. Once you have recognized what the negative self-talk is, practise coming up with a replacement solution that gets you focused on taking positive action, rather than dwelling on the negative possibilities.

We have provided a couple of charts that outline the specific challenge of combating negative self-talk. To begin with, though, you might want to get a set of typical negative statements identified that are relevant to you, or the player you are working with. Once you have identified these negative statements, you can practise using the charts to help reframe the statements.

The first question you need to answer, though, is 'How good are you at recognizing when you're saying the wrong thing to yourself?' The Steve Redgrave quote shows how well he could do this even at the most critical times. There's no denial of the negative thinking, but a very strong ability to change the potentially destructive thoughts around.

Once you recognize this negative thinking, you do have to be able to give yourself the 'mental slap'. Psychologists refer to this as

Change From . . .	Change To . . .
I don't ever have a good game when this guy refs, he's always got it in for me.	I won't let this ref put me off . . . to be the best I have to be able to play well whoever's reffing.
I worried about keeping my place . . . the new signing looks like a real threat to me.	I'm good under pressure . . . keeping playing to your strengths and the boss won't be able to drop you.
What a stupid mistake . . . I can't believe I did that.	Everyone makes mistakes . . . it's how you respond that's important . . . positive with the next possession.
We're just not getting the run of the ball today… I can't believe how unlucky we're being.	Keep positive, keep focused on using the ball well, we'll make our own luck by staying positive.
I know I'm being watched today, I hope I don't have a bad game.	You're being watched because you're good, so keep doing the things that made them want to watch you in the first place.

Negative	Positive
'It's difficult for me . . .'	*'It's a challenge for me . . .'*
'I can't . . .'	*'I can . . . if/provided I . . .'*
'If only . . .' 'I hope that . . .'	*'When . . .'*
'If I . . .'	*'When I . . .'*
'I'm worried about . . .'	*'I'll be O.K. . . . if . . .'*

thought-stopping, which can be a really helpful technique. The thought stopping is a mental cue that is used to block out the negative thoughts. So, on recognizing the presence of the negative thoughts, an image or word is used in the mind to stop the negative thoughts coming through. The choice of image or word is completely individual, but obvious images that have worked well are large red traffic lights, a large STOP road-sign, a road-block or a big emergency stop button on electrical equipment. Unsurprisingly, saying stop! to yourself, in your head or out loud, is a simple reminder to halt the negative thoughts. The word or image can be effectively paired up with a physical cue being used at the same time. So, as well as stopping the thought in the head, a clenched fist, clapping hands together sharply, or slapping your thigh, acts to get the focus back onto the positive thoughts as well.

Once the stop! has worked, this must then be swiftly followed up with the positive statement that gets the player focused very firmly on the positive action that will follow. Not bringing in the positive focus can result in the negative thought coming back as it has not been dealt with.

Don't Say That!

Within self-talk there is a special case for singling out the word 'don't' for some special treatment. If you say to a player (or they say to themselves) 'Don't miss a tackle in the final third', then the brain receives a message of what 'not' to do, but is not given a clear positive instruction of what action needs to be taken. The 'don't' instruction has generated an unnecessary additional component in decision-making. Now, when in the final third and under attack from an opponent, the player's mind will go through the following: . . . so, the ***don't*** instruction has brought in delays to the decision-making process, images of the undesired action, a delay in actually

Positive Self-Talk

The classic example is the weekend golfer faced with a simple wedge to the green. 'Don't lift your head', he says. 'Don't go in the water. Don't do what you did last week', he exhorts to himself as he addresses the ball . . . the result? – Surprise, surprise – head up, a topped shot and the ball squirts into the lake!

The accomplished golfer on the other hand uses positive self-talk when faced with the same shot. 'Head still, swing slow, middle of the green' are the focusing thoughts as the ball is being addressed . . . result? A steady shot over the water and onto the green safely.

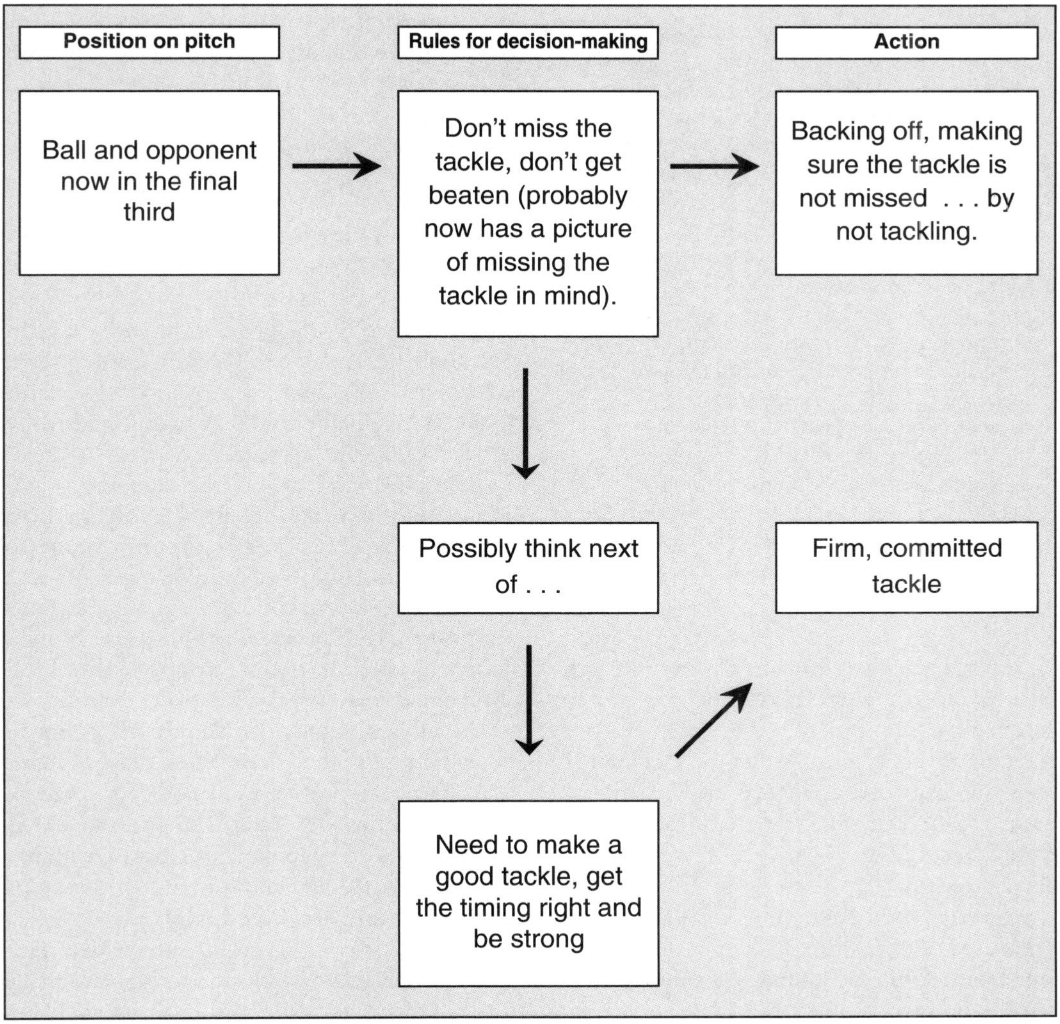
Position on pitch
Rules for decision-making
Action
Ball and opponent now in the final third
Don't miss the tackle, don't get beaten (probably now has a picture of missing the tackle in mind).
Backing off, making sure the tackle is not missed . . . by not tackling.
Possibly think next of . . .
Firm, committed tackle
Need to make a good tackle, get the timing right and be strong

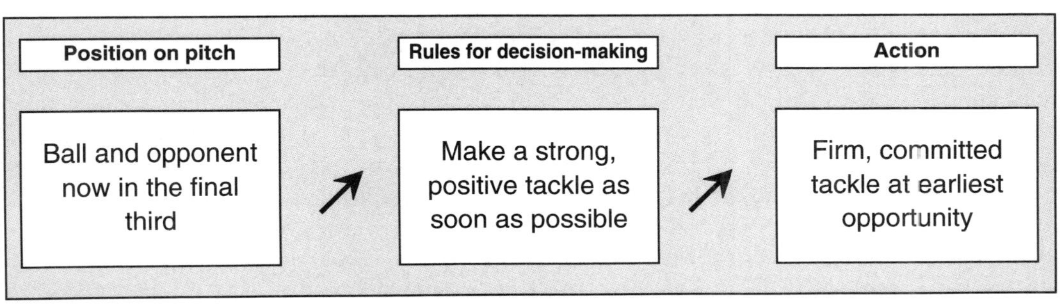
Position on pitch
Rules for decision-making
Action
Ball and opponent now in the final third
Make a strong, positive tackle as soon as possible
Firm, committed tackle at earliest opportunity

> This feeling of inferiority definitely affected my performance. I always worried what the other Scotland players would think if I had made a mistake. I feared they would believe I had let them down, that I should be able to do better, that someone else could do better than me, that I should be dropped. All those questions tugged at my concentration. It was self-destructive on my part. I shouldn't have been like that. There were fellow squad members who I could have talked to about the problem, like George Graham and Bruce Rioch, both people you could have an intelligent conversation with, but I never felt able to broach the subject of my inferiority. I was too embarrassed too discuss it.
>
> **Kenny Dalglish**
> (*Dalglish: My Autobiography*, 1996)

tackling. The player is probably worried about failing, as opposed to being focused on succeeding. It is possible that the player may even be thinking 'Don't miss the tackle or the boss is going to come down on you after the game.' You can imagine that the situation would become even worse if a tackle is actually missed.

Consider how their mindset differs when the instruction provided is, 'as soon as you're faced with someone taking you on in the final third, get a strong, positive tackle in as early as possible'.

The absence of the 'don't', or more importantly the presence of a positive instruction, speeds up the decision-making process, and allows the player to be focused on making sure of some positive action. They are clear in their mind what is expected of them, so are not caught in two minds, and are not second-guessing themselves.

So, make sure you use a lot of positive instructions. Send players out with positive instructions, not negative ones. The language we use with players quickly becomes the language they use to themselves, so it is critical to monitor your use of words in instructions that you give if you want to make sure that their head is full of the right self-talk when they are out on the pitch.

ACT CONFIDENT . . . PLAY CONFIDENT

Although we'd always recommend the self-talk and thought-control techniques to stay as confident as possible, there is another variable that can be equally useful in taking control to really stack the confidence odds in your favour. Our body, body language and physiology play a very important role in how confident we feel. It's really important to recognize the type of body language that accompanies being confident. If our thoughts are positive, but everything about our body is acting negatively (head dropped, shoulders slouched, avoiding eye contact, moving lethargically), then unsurprisingly it's going to be difficult for the thoughts to have a long-lasting impact. Therefore, we have to practise changing our body language to help either kick-start or complement our positive thinking. Players need to know what positive body language is and act accordingly.

A useful way of deciding how body language needs to be positive is to identify a role model who has excellent body language. You can usually look at top players as good examples of helpful body language. Think of Alan Shearer with penalties, or Roy Keane when he is controlling the midfield. From a goalkeeping perspective, there is no better example than Peter Schmeichel at the top of his game. The posture of these players, their movement, eye contact and gestures are all very positive, and these positive behaviours would certainly match up with positive thoughts underneath.

You can encourage players to take on the body language of key role models at critical moments in games, or merely as part of their consistent preparation for matches. Once a role model has been identified, it is easy to try to emulate them, and benefit from the confidence they have developed in their game. Identify who you would like to use as a model to really help develop the positive, optimistic, professional attitudes that go hand in hand with confident performance.

To conclude this section, overleaf is a confidence planner chart that captures the essence of what we're advising you to do. Examine the sample chart and then consider how you might adapt it for your personal use by completing the blank one.

In short, we know that success breeds confidence, but we also know that confidence breeds success. Take personal responsibility for your self-belief and you'll be surprised at the results!

Confidence Planner

Best Performance Memories – Last Season

❑ The 2 goals I scored last season to secure our place in the cup final.

❑ Having one chance in the first team and not losing my place after that game.

❑ My free-kick that curled into the top corner – sweet strike!

❑ My end of season meeting with the gaffer – excellent things he said to me.

Self-talk Check

Change from: ⟶	*Change to:-*
I hope I don't lose the scoring touch.	Relax and trust your natural instincts.
I just can't beat players one on one at the moment.	Keep taking people on – pressure will tell.

What if another striker joins us this season? Remember the positives from the gaffer.

My controllables

❑ I can control how I prepare for matches and the mindset I bring to the changing room.

❑ I can control my diet and fitness training – I'll be the best prepared of the team.

❑ I can control my reactions to bad decisions – get focused back on the game.

Ideal player modelling

Think about how Alan Shearer would react and deal with a few games without a goal.

Look at the way Renaldo stays focused even when he's being kicked all over the place.

Always remember . . .

I'm fitter and better prepared than ever before - the results will follow.

Confidence Planner

Best Performance Memories

❑

❑

❑

❑

Self-talk Check

Change from: ⟶ *Change to:-*

My controllables

❑

❑

❑

Ideal player modelling

Always remember . . .

STEP 3

Mental Practice and Visualization

> The power of the mind really is incredible.
>
> **Sven-Goran Eriksson** (*Sven-Goran Erikkson on Football*, 2002)

The term 'visualization' is commonly used by sport psychologists and is one of the most useful mind skills that you can encourage your players to develop. It is an everyday skill that is used (as the examples throughout this section illustrate) by chefs, cab drivers, politicians and doctors as well as performers in sport, the opera and ballet. In this chapter we'll give you a clear description of what visualization is, how you can develop visualization skills, as well as various ways in which you can make use of visualization as part of mental preparation for football.

WHAT IS VISUALIZATION?

The examples in the box of visualization being used 'in performance' give us a useful initial insight into what it's all about. All of us have the ability to create or recreate images in our mind. Whether we are imagining a previous event, or thinking through an event that is just about to happen, our mind can create very clear pictures of us, our actions and our surroundings. If we take control of these pictures in our mind they can become a very useful component of mental preparation for sport. Although most players do use visualization regularly in an 'unplanned' way, they are not necessarily developing the skill as effectively as they could, and therefore, probably not getting maximum benefit from it. As with any skill, regular, deliberate practice improves the visualization skill, and therefore allows the player to get maximum benefit from it. So, if you take nothing else

> You can see the skill of visualization being used in many different sports:
>
> - Jonny Wilkinson during his conversion routine can be seen visualizing the ball being struck through the posts before actually kicking.
> - Watch David Beckham pause and focus prior to striking a free-kick as he readies himself.
> - Michael Schumacher sitting in the car, in the pit, eyes closed, rehearsing the detail of the lap in his mind as he prepares to race for qualification.
> - When playing international cricket, you would see Nasser Hussain and Michael Atherton out in the middle of the pitch, the day before a Test Match, visualizing facing the opposition, preparing themselves for the battle ahead.
> - Watch Tiger Woods as he stands behind his ball, putting, or driving, and you'll see him pausing as he creates an image in his mind of the shot he is about to play.

> Teddy's got an awareness of whether he should use the ball early or calm it down. He's got a picture in his head before the ball comes.
>
> **Peter Beardsley** talking about England footballer Teddy Sheringham (*The Daily Telegraph*, 27/5/98)

from this section, remember that visualization has to be practised in order for it to be effective.

The pictures that we can create can go well beyond just 'seeing' in the mind's eye. With regularly practised visualization it is possible to bring in an influence from all of the senses, with the images including hearing, smelling,

Different uses of visualization for football

Style of Use	*Example in action*
Practising specific skills in the mind	Rehearsing a Cruyff-turn with your weaker foot. Rehearsing strike of ball to increase amount of dip from a dead ball.
Improving confidence and positive thinking	Replaying career highlight moments in your mind. Seeing yourself playing well against a specific opponent.
Rehearsing tactics or problem-solving	Running through free-kick routines. Rehearsing in your mind how to break down a defence.
Controlling pre-match nerves (see STEP 5)	Focusing on images of playing well and playing positively. Replacing potentially negative images of what might happen, with positive images of what 'will' happen.
Match review and analysis	Replaying elements of match performances to help identify positive and negative points.
Match preparation (see STEP 7)	Visualization of playing at the ground you are going to be playing at. Immersing yourself in the environment of the ground. Seeing yourself playing there in different conditions, in different match situations.
Part of skill execution routines (see STEP 4)	As part of a penalty or free-kick-taking routine – visualizing confidently and positively striking the ball into the area of the goal that has been selected.
Maintaining mental freshness during injury (see STEP 7)	Imaging skills and tactics while out injured to keep the mind focused on match-related thinking.

tasting, and most important of all, for the sports performer, feeling. The feeling refers to emotions and physical sensations, and it is the physical component, or kinaesthetic element, that is probably the key to really effective visualization.

So, in essence, visualization is the reproduction in the mind of all the relevant sensory information that contributes to the successful execution of a skill, or the correct response for a specific situation. The regular use of visualization can really add another dimension to players' training and match preparation. The table on page 65 outlines the different uses of visualization available to use in football.

If you want to know which your natural visualization approach is, close your eyes and have someone draw a clock-face on your forehead and then get them to draw a time on the clock-face. Let's imagine that your friend draws the time on the clock that is shown in the example below. With your eyes shut and just feeling this, rather than seeing it, you might give one of two answers. If you say 3 o'clock, chances are that your preference is for 'outside' visualization – you have come outside yourself and watched your friend draw the time on your forehead from above or from the side, so giving the 3.00 o'clock response. Some people see (and say) 9 o'clock suggesting an 'inside' preference, as they have been looking 'out onto' the clock face as if it were directly in front of them. These people 'see' the clock hands being drawn down and to the left on the clock face, thus giving the 9.00 o'clock time.

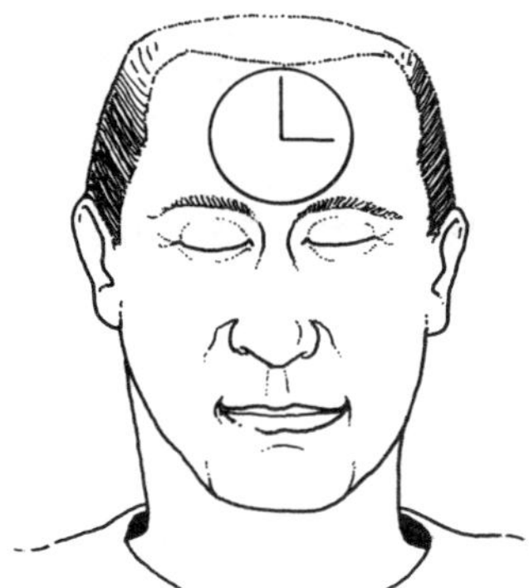

INSIDE OR OUTSIDE?

Whether you're using visualization as part of skill execution or for improving confidence, there are differences in what you might actually see, as we have different personal preferences for what we see. On the one hand, some players will prefer to visualize from the 'internal' perspective, or 'inside' style. This means that when they create a picture in their mind's eye, it is created from the perspective of what they actually see through their eyes when they are looking out on the world. This contrasts with the 'external', or 'outside' perspective. With the external perspective, the player creates a picture in their mind that is akin to watching themselves on a TV screen. Therefore, they are effectively watching themselves in their mind's eye or from a bird's eye view.

We are all able to switch between inside and outside visualization, but we do have a perspective that we naturally choose to use, and the clock face exercise will show you this. There is not right or wrong perspective, but it is thought that the inside perspective allows players to more easily develop a better quality of the 'feel' component. The outside perspective, on the other hand, is often thought to be particularly useful in helping to focus on tactical visualization, as well as being a good perspective to take when reviewing performances and objectively assessing quality of play.

Regular practice of visualization really helps to develop the ability to use both inside and outside perspectives, and players can then assess for themselves which is the most effective approach for them with the different uses of visualization training.

Interesting Uses for Visualization!

The laughing mouth is another mind game. I imagine a huge laughing mouth right behind the posts and that's someone smiling at me saying: 'You're having a bad day, there's no way you can make this kick, you're going to miss, you're going to keep missing all day.' The idea is to silence the laughing mouth by hitting the ball right into the back of its throat . . . This is all about dominating the kick, taking control of it and not letting it take control of you.

Jonny Wilkinson
(*The Times*, 2003)

We'll now provide you with a brief insight into the key uses of visualization so you can begin to build up a picture of the specific ways in which these approaches can help out. We'll also give you some explanations as to how and why the skill actually works and can help improve performance. You'll see in some of the other sections of the book that the other uses of visualization are highlighted, and because there are so many applications of the skill, you will quickly begin to appreciate why it's so important, but often so under-exploited.

BUILDING AND MAINTAINING CONFIDENCE

You've already seen the extensive amount of ideas about confidence in Step 2, and some initial ideas about using visualization to help with building and maintaining confidence. Having identified performance highlights as part of the reminders process you have instantly got a great start for confidence-building visualization. Repeating the positive statements can be very effective for some players. However, many players we have talked to get a really positive impact from actually visualizing the events associated with the statements. Therefore, rather than just saying the statements, we encourage these players to regularly repeat the images of success and achievement in their mind. They can recall or create all of the positive emotions associated with performing to the best of their ability, and use these positive feelings to help develop a positive view of themselves and how they want to play in matches. The player is obviously recalling or creating positive actions as well as emotions, so there is a very powerful combination of thoughts and feelings being focused upon. This really helps to get the balance evened up between the amount of positive and negative images that we have in our head. It can be useful to think of visualization as a personal library of video clips that you can dip into as regularly as you like. Obviously, the more regularly you use the library, the more this will help with confidence and positive attitudes.

Although we have stressed the importance of focusing on process goals, football is obviously about winning and achieving success. Therefore, from a motivational perspective, visualization is very useful in giving players the opportunity to see and experience success in their mind's eye. This helps on two fronts. First, the player focuses on the motivating emotions of winning, being successful, beating key opponents, lifting trophies – the competitive reasons that drive us. Second, by visualizing these successful outcomes, players improve their positive mental attitude, and become more used to seeing themselves in winning situations. This ability to see yourself as a winner is part and parcel of developing a confident, winning mindset, so there is definitely a place for this outcome-focused visualization from time to time.

Obviously, as well as this outcome-focused visualization, it is important to build confidence by actually visualizing executing processes effectively in game situations. This is particularly useful for players in the lead-up to

The best players in the world are able to use visualization as part of their training and preparation. ©EMPICS/ ZUMA Press

matches, particularly if they are prone to getting very nervous or getting excessively focused on worrying about what might happen in a match. If the nerves, or questions about the match can be answered with positive images of the player performing well, in different conditions, different times of the game, against different individual opponents, then the player becomes used to focusing on how they intend to play, rather than focusing upon unanswerable questions.

We often talk to players about making sure they are developing the confidence that they can be a consistent performer across a variety

Interesting uses of Visualization!

Visualizing myself in the Commons giving my maiden speech made me so nervous that I sat down at my PC and began shaking. Every time I visualized standing up in the chamber my heart started racing. But I visualized the whole thing through, including my movements and gestures; I'm sure that made it better. The best speeches are those where the speaker is visualizing something powerful as they talk.

Lembit Opik, Liberal Democrat MP

of different situations, and this varied visualization really helps the players focus on performing to their strengths regardless of the situation they are playing in. This idea of being confident in yourself, whatever the circumstances is essential to work towards if players are going to build the unshakeable confidence that we talked about in Step 2.

We've found it useful to get players to identify different situations to help with developing an unshakeable confidence. The first scenario requires the player to identify the conditions that they would choose to play in every week, if they could choose – weather, pitch, opposition, time of day, crowd size, and referee. Once they have identified these elements, they then need to identify what they would be thinking, how they would be feeling (emotionally), what they would be saying to themselves, what their body language would be like, and what the opposition would be thinking seeing them in this positive situation. With this detailed information, we then challenge the player to describe their least preferred, most challenging set of circumstances to play in. With this context now clear in their mind, they are challenged to visualize themselves playing with the same set of thoughts, feelings and actions that they previously said would result from their 'perfect day' scenario. This simple exercise gets the player used to seeing themselves performing in the ideal mindset in less than ideal circumstances, and recognizing that whatever is going on around them, they are in charge of managing their mindset – *they know that they control the situation, the situation does not control them*, and the visualization of this process of taking control provides a crucial confidence building block.

Some players have also found it useful to identify role models to help with developing visualization of playing in a very confident manner. By identifying a player, or several players who are thought to be good confidence role models, it is then possible to visualize yourself performing with their characteristics, and their confidence. It is easy to identify how they would respond and portray themselves in a variety of situations, and once this has been achieved, the player can carry out good quality visualization sessions with the aim of seeing themselves responding and acting with the confidence and assurance of the role models. In time, the player begins to associate themself with these positive responses, rather than with the role model.

Practice Exerise

1. Identify a specific situation in which you want to perform better.
2. Visualize the situation in as much detail as possible including – weather, pitch, crowd noise, state of the game, etc.
3. Visualize how you want to be feeling, what you want to be thinking and the body language you wish to portray.
4. Visualize successful performance – pay attention to what it feels like to execute with confidence.

PRACTISING SPECIFIC SKILLS IN THE MIND

It's really helpful when thinking about improving skill to bear in mind that skill is actually controlled by the brain, and therefore the secret to changing and maintaining skill is to ensure that the brain is 'reprogrammed' with new instructions. Once these new instructions are in place, it is much more likely that the body will readily reproduce the new pattern. Practice without reprogramming the brain will lead to a player sporadically showing they can execute the new skill pattern, but under pressure they will actually revert to their old habits. So whether you are looking to slightly change the way a dead ball is being struck, develop a new trick for beating a defender, or improve the way a player is attacking the ball with their head, then the visualization needs to become a central element of the process.

There is a vast amount of scientific research that shows when it comes to helping an athlete to develop skill, the best way to bring this about is through a combination of actual physical practice with consistent visualization. The physical practice ensures that body and mind are getting used to working in harmony to produce the slightly different pattern of skill. This is then complemented by the visualization sessions that ensure that the brain is beginning to restructure the subtle ways in which messages are sent to the muscles in order to produce the skill. All skill relies upon having a set of rules in the memory that the brain refers to when the skill needs to be executed, and the more quickly the new programme can overwrite the old one, the better. Once again, although we are talking about visualization, perhaps the most important element in helping implant the new programme is the feel component of the skill. Therefore, this means that the combination of physical practice and visualization becomes even more important, due to the necessity to very specifically identify the critical bits of physical feedback that tell the player they have got the skill correct. These physical cues may relate to balance, rhythm of movement, body position, acceleration of body, or lightness of movement – the key is to encourage your players to identify exact detail to be used during the visualization.

The evidence from the research laboratories is compelling, with many experiments showing that when a sports performer visualizes the picture and the feel of a movement, there is electrical activity taking place in the muscles that is associated with the movement. Therefore, the brain is actually mimicking firing the muscles in the patterns that are needed to execute the skill, but at a level that is not quite enough to make the actual body part move.

Not only does the visualization help with putting in place the new control programme, but you can imagine that the more you actually 'see' and feel yourself carrying out a skill successfully, the more you will be likely to carry it out effectively in reality. The simple rehearsal of the skill in the mind lays down a picture of positive expectations, so the player has a positive perception of their ability to carry it out, and therefore is relaxed and confident about it. Contrast this with the player who constantly replays mistakes in his or her mind, and repeatedly tenses up when in that situation, so increasing the likelihood of that mistake recurring. The relationship works so well in the negative version, we might as well turn things in our favour and get this working for us in a positive sense . . . once again, taking

Research at the Cleveland Clinic Foundation in Ohio

Ten volunteers who took part in mental workouts five times a week, imagining lifting heavy weights with their arms, increased their bicep strength by 13.5 per cent and maintained the increase for 3 months after the training stopped

Reported in *New Scientist* (2001) – **G. Yue**

Interesting Uses for Visualization!

Every chef uses visualization. You have to visualize what you're going to put on the plate before you do it. I visualize the completed thing, then work back mentally, thinking and visualizing textures and contrasts . . . I cook from noon to 3pm and from 7 to 11pm, and it's usually then, at the height of things, that I visualize, and create the best dishes.

Gordon Ramsay

control of our mind and our thinking to ensure that every possible advantage is being pursued.

If you have a new player coming into your side and you play a different formation, or are going to require them to play a slightly different tactical role from the one they are used to, then the visualization can work in exactly the same way as with the skill development. With regular visualization of themselves playing in the new role or formation, they can put in a good amount of time 'on the pitch' in their mind. So, rather than waiting for practice situations or match situations to help get used to the new role, they develop their awareness of the new demands by structured 'mental training' sessions. The sessions don't have to be as long as training sessions or matches, and of course the player does not need to rely upon all the other players to be around to help them get used to the new tactics. As with the skill related visualization, this approach works by helping to speed up the learning process, and helping the player to develop a new 'blueprint' in their mind.

Interesting Uses for Visualization!

When you do The Knowledge they tell you that one day you'll wake up and see the streets in your head. The Knowledge is all about visualization. I used to drive around on a bike with a clipboard on the front. When I got home I'd sit in a room and go over the runs that I'd done. I'd visualize the streets in my head, seeing all the landmarks and the cars parked on the roadside to get a real picture. It's no good just going over the run with a map; you want a picture of what you'll see when you're really doing the route.

Garry Slattery, London cab driver

MATCH REVIEW AND ANALYSIS

Most of the visualization suggested so far has focused on helping to influence performance in the future. However, the skill of visualization can be just as useful after a match is over, and evaluation of performance needs to take place. Obviously, being able to look back over a match video is the ideal way of appraising the positives and negatives from performance, but not every player has the time or opportunity to engage in this detail. As we effectively have a 'recording' of the match in our head, this is where the visualization can be really helpful. We've already highlighted the importance of match reviews in relation to confidence-building, and this can be made easier to complete if visualization is used post-match.

Whenever you decide that you are going to carry out your review, scan through the images of the game in your head, and make a note of which key phases of the game come to mind. These will normally be the positive and negative elements of the game, but try to make sure you at least get a balance between the two. The aim of specifically identifying these images and dealing with them in a structured way can be a great help in keeping a positive sense of progress. Rather than frequently pondering on the negatives and positives over the course of a couple of days, the structured use of the visualization in combination with the review allows the images to be used effectively to help give direction and purpose in training. Of course, the identification of the key positive images is really helpful in adding to your growing visualization highlight list, and you make sure you get an accurate, constantly updated set of experiences to draw upon.

Another element to the recording of these images relates to planning for the future. With a detailed record of the positive experiences that have taken place within a specific match you can then look back at the review ahead of the next game at that ground or against that opposition. So, during the build-up to the match you know that you are going to be bringing to mind the key positive reminders that will help maximize your confidence for the game. Therefore, you get the benefit of using both general positive visualization and opponent/ground specific content to shape your mindset as you approach a match.

TOP TIPS FOR MAXIMIZING QUALITY OF VISUALIZATION

As with any kind of training, you can carry out visualization with varying degrees of quality. If you follow the ideas below, you'll ensure that the visualization that is engaged in is given the best chance of being effective. Remember, visualization is a skill, so the more it is practised the better you become at it, and the more impact it will have on mind and body. Therefore, it's worth giving the your visualization the best chance of developing quickly by getting the basics in place from the start. As the skill develops, it might be possible to experiment some more with the different recommendations to see if you can get any more quality out of the session.

1. Mental Warm-Up

The mental warm-up consists of making sure that you know the exact purpose of the visualization session, and how long you are going to spend visualizing. Once you know the purpose of the session, you'll have clearly identified the images that you need to play through, and what you need to say to yourself. Having identified the images, it'll also be important to make sure that the 'feel' elements are clearly outlined too, where they are needed.

If possible, make sure you are not going to be interrupted part way through your session. To begin with, it is likely that concentration will be hard to maintain, so avoiding unnecessary distractions is helpful. In time, you might not be so concerned with distractions as it will be much easier for you to maintain concentration and quality of visualization. Eventually, it should be possible to carry out visualization in the noisy atmosphere of changing rooms, should you feel it appropriate.

When you are ready to start the visualization, select a position that allows you to get the best quality visualization. This might be sitting or standing, but experiment to find out if different body positions give you different quality to your sessions. Once in a comfortable position, close your eyes (although some people find eyes open more effective), and focus on getting your body into a state that you would associate with playing – you want to make sure you are tension free, but feeling as alert, focused and ready as you would in the real life scenario. Spend a minute or so getting into the right state. Once you are there, your body and mind should now be appropriately switched on for visualizing the chosen content of your session.

2. Use All the Senses . . . but Make Sure You *Feel* It!

Although we made this point right at the beginning of the section, it's worth re-stressing. Some senses are of course more relevant than others, but it seems that sounds can be particularly important. This would certainly be the case for helping to bring the emotional side of the visualization to the fore – if a player can imagine the crowd noise, the thumping sound of a fiercely struck shot, or the words being said to a player, then this can really help to make the images very vivid and emotionally charged.

It's a little obvious to suggest visualizing in colour, but do make sure that this is an important part of the content. As controllability and quality of the visualization improve, then quality of the pictures will improve, and colours will become sharper, and the whole image more realistic. When beginning the

> **Interesting Uses for Visualization!**
>
> When you put a needle into a vein, often you can't see it. You have the markings that you have been taught in anatomy, but you have to visualize beyond that. With an abdominal problem you have to envisage what the abdomen and the ruptured cells look like. It's very important when you're doing a procedure like an endoscopy.
>
> **Kevin Gunning**, Consultant anaesthetist

visualization training, it's worth keeping some scores out of ten for the quality of the sensory elements. You'll soon get a feel for how well you use the different senses and produce colours, and you'll then be able to emphasise the key senses that you need to work on improving within the sessions.

Although we'd encourage all the senses to be used, as you've already realized, we would promote the importance of 'feel' or kinaesthetic components more than any other. The quality of feel can really be assisted by concentrating upon things such as balance, weight movement, and feel of the ground underfoot. It can also be helpful to focus on actually being in your playing kit, identifying what the fabrics feel like, and how comfortable your boots are, and so on. This detail really helps the brain recall images from within the memory stores, which in turn ensures a good quality picture in the mind's eye. If it helps, it can even be worth putting kit and boots on to really help create a vivid picture. You're only one step short of actually physically practising now, but with the visualization, you obviously don't have to deal with getting physically tired as a result of repeated practice, and you don't have to clean your boots!!

3. Real Time

Visualizing in 'real-time' is very important for the quality of your session. Whatever you have chosen to visualize, aim to go through the pictures in your mind at the speed at which they would actually happen were you experiencing them for real. For example, in timed sports, the athletes are able to visualize their performance to within fractions of a second, so their mind is being prepared as realistically as possible to face the challenges of the real life situation. Running through a skill, or situation too fast or too slow will probably not give the full benefit as decision-making, movement patterns, reaction times and physical components are not actually being considered in a reliable manner.

Visualizing in real time is not an easy task, so make sure this element of the quality of the training is taken seriously. If you need convincing that it's not easy, visualize yourself walking a familiar route that you use regularly. It might be from the car park at the training ground into the changing rooms. Time how long this takes you when you visualize it, and next time you do the walk for real, check the real time. You may be surprised by the results. If you want to try it with more performance-related activities, then visualize yourself going through your penalty routine (see Step 4); time how long it takes from placing the ball on the spot to the point when it is struck, and then get someone to time your routine for real.

We'd certainly recommend that you use video or DVD to help get the real-time element of the visualization as good as possible, especially when you are visualizing specific skills or movement patterns. By watching the skill on the screen first, you can then study the timing elements in detail before trying to replicate the experience in your mind's eye. If you don't get on well with visualizing, then it may be better to stick to using the video clips all the time. Recent research has shown that this can be just as effective as visualizing, providing that you imagine being inside the image that is on the screen, rather than just watching it as a removed viewer . . .

you have to try to re-experience the image on the screen!

Simply, identify the sequence or skill that is going to be visualized. Play the sequence on the video or DVD, pause it, and then visualize the same sequence, focusing on creating all of the sensory feedback that you would associate with what has just been watched. Therefore, if a player is using the role modelling approach, they would substitute themselves into the scene, and feel themselves performing in exactly the same way that they have just seen their role model perform. Having visualized, the clip is then played again to assess the accuracy and quality of the visualized version. This process can be completed ten to fifteen times in a session, which will really give the player a good opportunity to enhance the quality and impact of the visualization.

4. Quality Sessions – Set Goals for Adherence

You need to build up the time of your sessions little by little in order to get the best quality visualization for as much of the session as possible. If you carry on sessions for too long, you can lose the quality of visualization and the session loses impact. Therefore, set yourself some time limits to begin with and focus on short but frequent sessions rather than longer sessions carried out less frequently. We would recommend that you give yourself a quality rating after each session to make sure that you are monitoring the clarity, quality and control of the sessions. So, get used to scoring a session out of 10 for how well you maintained focus and control of the images. You might also want to set yourself some targets for how frequently you will carry out sessions of specific lengths. In our experience, players don't stick to this kind of training very well, so you have to do something to make the importance of it stand out and the likelihood of the training being maintained maximized.

Using a simple visualization training diary is useful.

In the diary, you can review the sessions under the headings of:

Time of Day

Content of Session

Length of Session

Quality of Picture

Quality of Feel

Overall Satisfaction with Session

If you do this, you'll start to get a feel for how to get the most out of each session, and you'll even see if there are variations in the quality depending upon when you carry out the session and what you have concentrated upon.

THE CONCENTRATION BENEFIT

Visualizing regularly will actually have the added benefit of improving concentration ability. Obviously, in order to visualize, you are having to select very specific things for your mind to focus on, and you'll have to maintain the focus for the duration of your visualization session. By definition, you are then having to block out irrelevant information since you are practising concentration. We often have athletes telling us that the more they practise their visualization the better they are able to control their thinking and concentration in performance. This improvement shows in two key ways; first, in the ability to maintain concentration for a period of focused time, second, and more importantly, the players tell us that they have been able to improve on staying focused on the things that are really important in helping them play well. Too often, footballers, as well as all sports people, get distracted by focusing on things that just don't matter, or that they are not directly in control of . . . and the visualization often works as an excellent filter to really help players differentiate between those things that matter, and those that don't. So that is another benefit from regularly giving your visualization skills a work-out . . . and if concentration can be improved, there's no doubt that any team would believe that that can make a significant contribution to them becoming more successful.

We'll finish this section with another quote from Jonny Wilkinson that provides an excellent example of how visualization can directly impact on skill execution. Don't be afraid to be creative in your visualization methods!

> In 1998, before my first game as England fly half, there were problems. Nothing was coming together. Eventually Dave Alred, my kicking coach said: 'Forget about technique. Imagine a lady in the crowd behind the posts. Try to hit her.' So we did and she became known as Doris; we picked out a spot for her and tried to hit her. And then we imagined her reading a newspaper and we tried to kick that out of her hands. Later we imagined her with a can of Coke and we tried to hit that. The idea was that instead of aiming at the posts, you were aiming at something specific 30 yards back, changing the emphasis of where I was aiming. It made me really kick through the ball.
>
> **Jonny Wilkinson**

STEP 4

Focusing and Concentration

The team was much more focused on defending well. I felt the concentration was high even when it was difficult and that the team had the right attitude. I have been slightly concerned that when a game was going a bit one way or the other way, it went the other way. Of course that's down to concentration. I think the players realized that as well. You look at how you lose games and think you have to focus better.

Arsene Wenger (*The Guardian*, 23/12/02)

Concentration is the key to it, and our second-half concentration was better. You have just got to be aware of the counter-attack. For a long time I was preoccupied with my concentration during games.

If you are a striker and you lose concentration, you give away possession but at the back of your mind you know you'll get another chance. When you play at the back any loss of concentration – even for a few seconds – can be a problem . . . Any mistake can be punished.

Mikael Silvestre (www.4thegame.com, 2003)

These two opening quotes highlight the importance of concentration – both from a team perspective and an individual perspective. Arsene Wenger highlights the critical nature of concentration for actually helping win matches, and Mikael Silvestre outlines the importance of not making mistakes. It is interesting to note that Silvestre went on to say that he did not find a solution to his concentration problem, but that he simply waited for time and experience to add up and improve things. Imagine if Silvestre had made this statement about his heading ability . . . 'I knew heading for me was a problem, but I just waited until I got better at it.' Would a manager stand for this when it's possible to practise and improve heading, with simple approaches? The answer is definitely, 'no', and as concentration is a skill that can be enhanced, then it should be treated in exactly the same way as physical ability. This section will show you the simple ways in which players can focus on improving their concen-

Hornets' chief calls for more concentration

Watford boss Ray Lewington has admitted his side need to cut out the mistakes if they are to turn their season around.

The Hornets have only managed one league win in seven matches, and Lewington wants his players to work on their concentration.

He told the official club website: 'Let's cut out the unforced errors, battle our way through it and not let mistakes affect us on the pitch'.

tration, rather than simply hoping they'll be able to concentrate better at some point down the line.

These approaches would certainly have helped Ray Lewington's players to have some structured ways to respond to their manager's request for concentration improvements.

Concentration is really all about being in a relaxed state of alertness – you know what you need to focus your attention on, and you are focused on these cues. Equally, within concentration, players need to know what irrelevant cues are, and how to shut these out in order to focus solely upon those things that help with decision-making, speed of reaction or anticipation. We know within football that being able to concentrate for the full 90 minutes is critical, so we also have to appreciate that there is a need to manage concentration within a match so that at the critical times focus is at its best. The concentration demands are position specific, and so when working through this chapter, keep in mind how the critical cues differ from goalkeeper all the way through to the front players. Of equal importance with concentration is that fact that the demands differ within the game. For instance, for the majority of the game, players have to concentrate on open play and all of the various constantly changing cues that help them read the game. Contrast this with dead ball situations, where the point of play is fixed, and therefore concentration is quite different. You'll see how important it is to appreciate these different concentration demands and also account for natural differences in concentration style.

In order to actually manage concentration demands effectively players are constantly having to scan the playing environment, take note of relevant information, and filter out irrelevant information. Crucial moments can happen at any point in a game, so there is no room for switching off concentration when the ball is in play. Players need to be monitoring their focus throughout the game, ensuring that they are staying in the right zone of concentration for them, and not letting focus drift away from the key performance cues. These demands set the scene for the critical challenges of concentration. It's clear that players have to be able to:

- **Develop appropriate concentration in the lead-up to the game.**
- **Be able to recognize quickly within the game when concentration has been lost.**
- **Be able to regain concentration quickly when they recognize it has been lost.**
- **Be able to manage concentration throughout all the different phases of a game in order to keep it at its peak throughout 90 minutes or more.**

As an initial set of points, these four areas give you a reference point for how to start assessing concentration. You can use the following table to assess overall confidence and establish where concentration weaknesses might be by scoring each area out of 10.

Concentration Area	Score
1. Develop appropriate concentration in the lead-up to the game.	?/10
2. Be able to recognize quickly within the game when concentration has been lost.	?/10
3. Be able to regain concentration quickly when recognizing it has been lost.	?/10
4. Be able to manage concentration throughout all the different phases of a game in order to keep it at its peak throughout 90 minutes or more.	?/10
TOTAL	?/40

> Jussi is at the peak of his game. He has saved us in games and won us points. His performances have been crucial. He has not been all that busy because of our outstanding defensive qualities of late. But what he has had to do, he has done with skill, ability and excellent concentration. Concentration levels are crucial for a goalkeeper.
>
> **Sam Allardyce**
> (www.footballtransfers.info)

CONCENTRATE!!!! . . . ON WHAT?

The shout from the sidelines of 'Concentrate!' is more often than not a completely useless instruction, unless it has been agreed in advance exactly what the players have to focus their attention towards when they hear this command. If anything, the instruction is simply a message to the player/s that concentration has been lost (that is, they have stopped focusing on the things they should be focusing on), and that they need to regain appropriate focus. As we go through this section, you'll see that there are a great many things to consider before you can be fully confident that players will be able to respond to a comment to refocus effectively.

Different types of concentration exist in sport and performers vary in their ability to use each of them. An American psychologist, Robert Nideffer, developed a framework for examining attentional control that we have simplified and applied to football below. We've identified three basic forms of concentration – external broad; external narrow; internal. You need to be able to use each at different stages of a game.

External Broad: Scanning the field

This concentration style allows a player to take in a lot of information, and be paying attention to key pieces of information simultaneously. When David Beckham plays a 50yd cross-field ball, he has very quickly used an external broad concentration style to see where the defenders are, where his target man is, and decide where the ball needs to be delivered in order to set the target man free. Within the broad concentration style he may also have accounted for wind direction and how this would influence the way the ball needs to be struck.

External Narrow: Focusing on a target

This type of concentration allows a player to be very focused on very limited cues. For example, when a goalkeeper is facing a free-kick just outside the area, their focus is limited purely on the ball, and the players involved in the free-kick. You can see here how a goalkeeper needs to very specifically practise this type of concentration as it differs markedly from when they are defending in open play and having to read the play, communicate with defenders about movements of attackers, and be ready to respond quickly in case a through ball is put through behind the defence, which they have to then intercept.

Internal: Attending to your thoughts and feelings

Internal concentration is being carried out when you focus inside on your thoughts and feelings. Examples include visualizing a free kick, repeating a cue word, focusing on the position of the left foot or concentrating on a steady breathing rhythm.

These three types of concentration can also be used to explain different types of distraction as the box below explains.

With these different aspects to concentration, it's really important to appreciate that a player needs to be able to switch between them if they are going to be able to concentrate effectively for all the demands of the

Distractions

External broad: Being distracted by crowd noise, shouting from the bench or players running off the ball when they do not interfere with what you are trying to do.

External narrow: The goalkeeper moving when you're about to take a penalty or free kick.

Internal: Worrying thoughts, a painful muscle, the mistake you made twenty minutes ago, how tired your legs are feeling.

game. One moment a player needs to be reading the game and conditions using external broad, and the next, they need to switch to external narrow when they are one to one with a player closing down on them. The ball then goes out for a corner and they need to switch to an internal attention to calm themselves down and make sure they are fully switched on for marking their opponent, which is swiftly followed by the switch to narrow external again as they attend to the ball being placed by the corner flag in readiness for the cross to be delivered. If any of these switches don't happen effectively, then the player will lose half a yard and be playing catch-up. Most concentration errors occur when a player does not make the changes quickly enough, or does not realize they are stuck in one concentration style so they miss out on crucial information. So, players need to know which type of concentration is needed at certain times and then develop strategies to ensure that they are in the correct focus at the right time.

A PRACTICE SWITCHING EXERCISE

It's actually relatively easy to practise switching between the different types of concentration, and it's actually a good idea to try this out to see how good you are at it. Away from the training ground you can simply identify three different things to focus on that fit into each category. The idea then is to change your attention and hold it on one type of focus for a set period of time before changing to a different focus. In time you will become better at switching the focus, and will be able to hold your concentration for longer in each area. Simply looking out of a window to use an **external broad** view can be a start. Then, after a while, you can switch to a single item within that view to practise an **external narrow** focus. Just switch from the wider view to the single item to begin with. To help with the internal and external switching, you might do this as you're working out. To practise the external focus, concentrate on anything outside your body – block out any focus on your level of fatigue, perceptions of effort, or how you are feeling. Keep this external focus going until you decide to switch to an internal focus – bring your attention onto a specific muscle, or your breathing rhythm or perhaps heartbeat – focus totally on your reactions and ignore anything outside you.

There is also a simple drill that you can try at the training ground. This is easy to practise on your own. With a ball outside the penalty area, focus on the broad picture of the goal. Keep focused on this, then quickly switch to one single piece of the net, blocking out all other detail. Now switch to the ball on the ground in front of you and a specific part of the ball. Next switch to visualizing yourself striking the ball – notice the feelings that you would get as you placed your non-striking foot and then hit the ball sweetly. You can then strike the ball for real, and repeat the exercise. Simple, good practice, that stretches your mental skills as well as honing your ball-striking skills.

You can obviously experiment to see how you could bring switching exercises into more

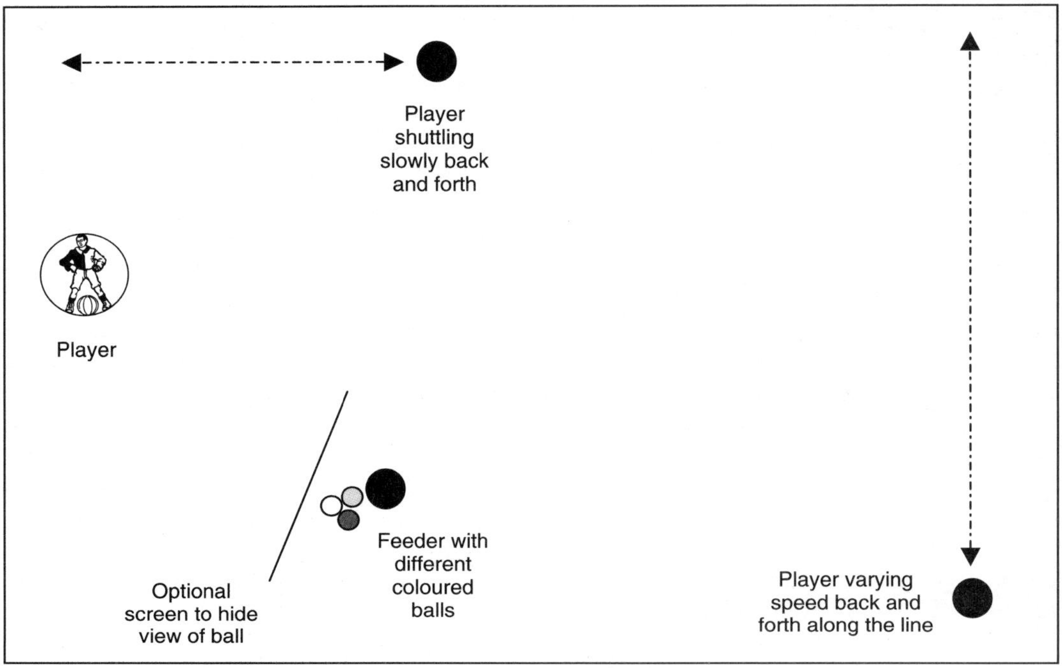

open practice situations. You could consider using different coloured balls in practice situations for example. There can be different rules for the different balls (yellow ball = instant 30yd pass to player on the move, white ball = control and pass to player moving away or towards you, red ball = control ball and return it to feeder with eyes closed). The diagram above shows how you might set this up and how the different concentration types are stretched. You can see that the player will have to practise switching focus between a broad and narrow perspective as well as an internal and external one as they have to respond to the different coloured balls coming to them. You can use different players to do the shuttle running so they don't get too tired. You might want to think about how you rotate players around the drill to get them concentrating under the pressure of fatigue having just run. Alternatively, you can have them coming into the exercise fresh. In this way, you can build up the demands of the task over time.

STAY IN CONTROL!

It's interesting to note that the more out of control players get in terms of how psyched up or how anxious they are, the more there is an impact on concentration. In short, focus of attention tends to narrow as we get more and more psyched up and energized. If we lose control of this process then it can go too far and result in a bad case of 'tunnel vision'. Think back to Paul Gascoigne's FA Cup Final tackle that led to him rupturing his cruciate ligaments. Gazza was clearly incredibly psyched up for the biggest game of his life, and his opening minutes of the game included two reckless tackles in areas of the pitch that didn't warrant such responses. His arousal levels had gone out of control, and his concentration and decision-making went out of the window. He was totally attentionally narrowed onto getting the ball at all costs, and lost concentration on his own safety, and how he needed to play in order to maximize his contribution to the team. If you get a chance to watch the opening minutes, it's an ideal example of how arousal level and concentration go hand in hand, and how important it is to make sure that players stay in control of their feelings and thoughts, in order to make sure they stay in control of their concentration. Contrast Gazza's state with how David Beckham recognized his anxiety and actively did something to regain control prior to taking the penalty against Argentina in the 2002 World Cup.

> I looked down at the ball before running up. It all went quiet. Everything was swirling around me, every nerve standing on edge. What's going on here? I can't breathe . . . I remember forcing in two big gulps of air to try and steady myself and take control.
>
> **David Beckham**
> (*David Beckham My Side*, 2003)

STAY IN THE PRESENT

One of the biggest challenges for concentration in football is to stay focused completely in the here and now. Before a match, the concentration wants to wander to the future to predict the result. During a match, concentration (our thoughts) often gets drawn to recent past events – maybe errors by yourself or others, or into the immediate future – thinking about how long is left and asking questions about what might happen. The more we dwell on these thoughts, and the more we are aware of them in our mind, the more concentration is taken away from what is actually happening in the here and now. Even a small decrease in concentration capacity can change performance, so the focus upon these thoughts can be damaging to performance. To focus on all of the information that needs taking in during a game, our attention does not have any room for wasted effort, so there is no room for taking up concentration space with an irrelevant focus.

> After missing an important penalty once, Jimmy Greaves turned to me as he trotted back to the centre and said 'Sometimes they go in and sometimes they don't.' He was one of the best at putting mistakes to the back of his mind.
>
> **Sir Geoff Hurst**

It's helpful for players to identify whether they are prone to losing their concentration in the past or future. Just simply identifying whether they focus on past events or future events can be a great help. Having identified where the typical loss of concentration lies, it is

Past ⟵	**Present**	⟶ **Future**
• Errors in the game. • Previous performances against opponent or at ground. • Missed opportunities. • Refereeing decisions.	• Focused only on a moment at a time approach. • The here and now.	• Focus on end of half or match with plenty of time still to play. • Thinking of selection to play for representative team if performance is good.

possible to be on the look-out for these self-imposed distractions and decide how to quickly bounce the focus back into the present.

ERRORS – DEALING WITH THEM EFFECTIVELY

Dealing with is possibly the most frequent internal distraction that we deal with, and it's important for players to have a routine they can go through in their mind to help make sure that error's life span does not last any longer than it needs to. It's important to be able to 'park' the error so that we stop thinking about it as quickly as possible, and get back to the here and now. The skill in 'parking errors' is to create an image in the mind that successfully removes the distraction and places the error somewhere in the mind where it is no longer interfering. Therefore, a player needs to find an image, or self-talk phrase, that is personally meaningful and effective. It's even possible to get the whole team to buy into error parking strategies, and in football this can be particularly helpful, as anyone can take the responsibility for helping players stay in the present and forget the past. We've found this kind of communication a great help to the mutual support within a team. In the box below are some examples of error parking strategies that have been used well.

Error Parking Examples

- In his head, a defender would put the image of the mistake inside a ball and kick it into touch.
- Another player imagined the scoreboard reading 'Never Make the Same Mistake Twice – get back in the game'.
- A central midfielder would simply imagine the mistake being put into a filing cabinet, knowing they could open it up after the game and think through what happened.
- A goalkeeper would imagine the errors going straight on a video recording so they could be watched after the game.
- A team decided that any errors were rubbish – they had happened and were no use any more – so when big errors were made someone would call 'bin it', to encourage the team to forget the error and move on.

Whatever the image or words are that you choose to act as an error parking technique, make sure that you actually practise using it, so that it becomes part and parcel of your in-game thinking. As training sessions can be just as pressurized sometimes, and we are more prone to make errors, it is essential to make sure that the error parking thoughts are used in training first of all – and don't forget, everyone makes mistakes, but it's the players that deal with them best who are the most consistent members of the team.

FIT BODY . . . FOCUSED MIND

One factor to always consider first and foremost with the players who you think struggle with concentration is that of the influence of the body on the mind. Physiology can influence a player's concentration in two ways. First, if a player is not fit enough, their energy

> I looked at Michael Owen. He had this aura about him, pure undiluted concentration on the job in hand.
>
> **David Beckham** commenting about Michael Owen immediately before the 2002 World Cup match against Argentina

will be disappearing towards the end of each half, and this makes the effort of actually concentrating much harder. It is likely that their fatigue will show through physically and mentally, and the silly mistakes associated with loss of concentration can come through. Mistakes at the end of each half can obviously have a significant impact on a match situation, so these losses of concentration become extra costly. So, one of the first things to consider with players who repeatedly lose concentration is their fitness. If you can count out the fitness variable, then you can take on the mental approach with greater confidence that it will bring a result.

The other body–mind factor to consider with concentration is that of nutrition. Often concentration can be made difficult because the brain is running low on fuel, so it's worth getting nutritional advice to make sure that brain and body are being fuelled properly for the full 90 minutes.

TAKING CONTROL OF CONCENTRATION

Think About What You Need to Think About!

The main principle to remember behind concentration is the idea that players *have to decide ahead of time what their thoughts need to be focused upon.* If a player has picked out the key things that they want to concentrate on, then it is easy for the mind to recall this in the game situation, and concentration becomes more readily achieved. If thought has not been given to how to create ideal focus ahead of the game, then when it comes to stepping over the white line, it is that much easier for the mind to become distracted. Therefore, if we come back to the shouted instruction of 'concentrate', this should actually become an instant reminder for a player about *what* to concentrate on, in keeping with what the player knows are the key concentration cues.

To help 'think about what needs thinking about', it's often useful to develop a simple concentration planner by answering the following questions:

- **Does concentration have a tendency to break down at similar points in a match?**
- **Is it particularly hard to maintain concentration in specific circumstances (opponent, stadium, floodlit, referee, etc.)?**
- **Are there critical times in matches when it is really important to make sure that concentration is at it's highest?**
- **How good is concentration at these critical moments?**
- **Consider your pre-match preparation for matches when you have been at your most concentrated. What kind of things were you thinking about and focusing on as you prepared for the match?**

When you have accurate answers to each of these questions, there is a strong basis for understanding how you need to go about choosing your approach to concentration. As you work through the remaining sections of this chapter, keep referring back to your answers to make sure you are putting the ideas into practice as effectively as possible. This will be a really effective way to exploit the strategies as there'll be a clear reference point on which to apply the ideas.

CONCENTRATION CUES

One of the most successful ways of focusing attention on the right things at the right time is through using personal concentration cues. Personal cues allow a player to intensify and relax concentration voluntarily, and need to be selected carefully and practised in training.

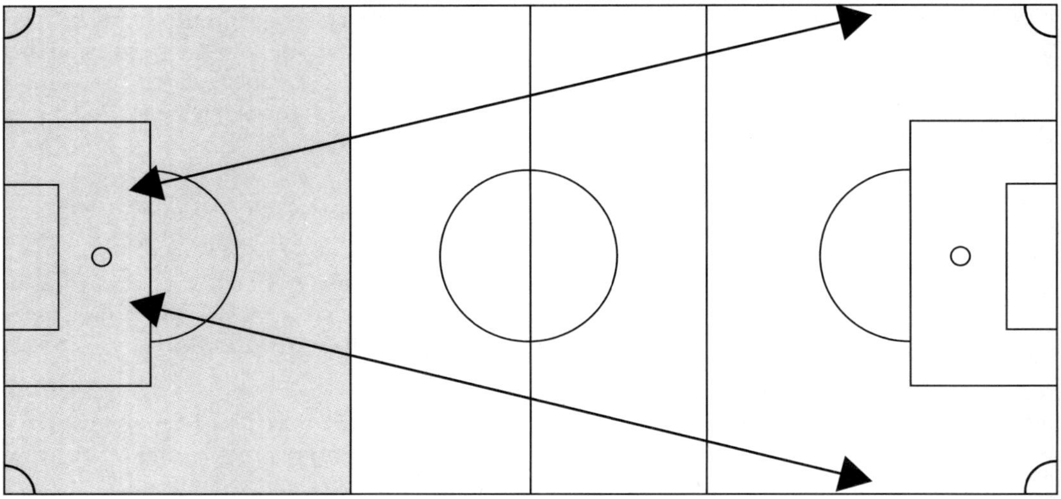

We'll go through the different types of concentration cue that can be used, but first, we'll give you the idea that concentration in matches needs to be thought of like a light switch, or volume control. Concentration needs to be able to be switched on and off, or up and down. It's impossible to stay a hundred per cent concentrated for the full 90 minutes of a match, as well as through half-time. The natural pattern of the game allows players to switch on and off, or up and down, so the concentration cues need to be applied within the structure of the game. Therefore, during injury breaks, times when the referee is talking to a player, or occasions when the ball is taking time to come back into play, there is an opportunity for players to relax concentration down before using their personal cue to switch back on to full game focus.

Players in specific positions can also manage concentration by switching up and down depending upon where they are on the pitch and where the ball is. A defender's concentration plan might look like the figure above. When the defender is in their final third of the pitch, and the ball is in the opposition's penalty area, concentration can be at a low, green, level. As the opposition move the ball into the middle third, concentration goes up a level, readying the player to act, and as the ball enters the defensive third, concentration is fully on (scanning the immediate environment for runs of attackers, clearly focused on the ball and the defender's position), and as the ball is cleared by a long defensive header, the concentration relaxes down again.

The structuring of the pitch to help with concentration is a very obvious and simple example of 'thinking about what you want to think about'. Players are obviously on the move the majority of the time during the course of the game, and the ball can move from attacking third to defensive third very quickly. Therefore, rather than thinking of switching confidence on and off, you might get a more positive reaction by challenging your players to be aware of *what* they need to concentrate on when play is in each different area of the pitch. The players can then use the different personal concentration cues to help them maintain appropriate concentration whenever the ball is in play.

The three key types of personal concentration cues are:

- Verbal cues
- Visual cues
- Physical cues

Example Physical Concentration Cues

Verbal:	'Eyes' 'Scan' 'Sharp, Sharp' 'Tracking'
Visual:	Placing the ball at a free-kick and focusing on manufacturer's name while readying self. *Checking position team mate while ball is in opponent's penalty area.*
Physical:	Re-tying laces while player gets treated for an injury. *Taking deep breaths as part of penalty routine.* Slapping cheeks or legs. *Opening and closing eyes in exaggerated manner as ball comes back into play.*

Cues That Could Work For Me

Verbal

Visual

Physical

Verbal concentration cues are usually a single word that the player repeats to him or herself as and when needed. This is focusing self-talk, and the words ensure that the mind is focusing on the key information.

Visual concentration cues involve focusing the eyes onto a specific object, and in turn this object reminds the player of the key concentration targets. Visual cues would normally be more useful when preparing for dead ball situations, as the visual cues tend to work best when they form part of a routine that is self-paced.

Physical cues involve carrying out any action that is associated with kicking off the concentration process. This kind of cue is probably most effective to help switch back on after there has been a break in play. The physical cue can be designed to make sure that the arousal levels are at the right level to most effectively influence concentration.

Some players just stick with one simple cue that helps them through all situations, and others use a combination of cues. The important thing with the cues is to make sure that the player makes decisions about when and how to use them, and then practises them regularly and consistently during training sessions. If the cues can be used to help a player achieve great focus in training, then they will certainly help achieve great focus during the more pressured competitive arena. With the regular training of concentration the cues eventually become automatic and less effort will be required to bring about a really focused in-match mindset. With an improved

> I have never ever protested to a referee about his decision because it is a waste of time and could destroy my concentration. If a player loses his temper with me and gets rough, I like it. It means he's the one who lost his concentration.
>
> **Sir Stanley Matthews**
> (*The Daily Mail*, 1/2/95)

<table>
<tr><th>Predictable Event</th><th>Normal, Distracting Response</th><th>Choose New, Refocusing Response</th></tr>
<tr><td>Referee makes a dubious decision.</td><td>Argue with referee, feel hard-done-by, dwell upon feelings of injustice, become angry and frustrated.</td><td>1. Say 'Stop' to self. Remind yourself you predicted the ref would make mistakes.
2. Sprint back in position immediately.
3. Take a deep breath and prepare to react quickly to win the ball back.</td></tr>
<tr><td colspan="3">All referees make mistakes, all players make mistakes. There's no point letting a referee's errors have a negative impact upon your performance by making you lose your focus. You can challenge yourself to reframe how you use the ref's mistake – for every mistake the ref make's this will help you check your concentration and make sure you are playing as well as possible.</td></tr>
<tr><td>Opponent constantly making offensive comments.</td><td>Make comments back, become angry at the comments, seek to enter into a physical battle with the opponent – losing sight of how you contribute best.</td><td>1. Say 'Confidence' to self. He's trying to distract you because you're a threat.
2. Focus back on personal targets for the match.</td></tr>
<tr><td colspan="3">stream of concentration cues... keep smiling at them and thanking them for helping you stay on your game!</td></tr>
</table>

natural concentration level, performance consistency normally results, and players are capable of responding quickly and with conviction at the critical moments.

We see many players who become excessively distracted by refereeing decisions and verbal exchanges with opponents. As opponents, this would be a positive sign for us to put more pressure on these 'distracted' players as they are not concentrating on the key factors that control their performance. For players who have trouble with these parts of the game, we would definitely recommend developing specific concentration routines. Certain events are very predictable, and if these predictable events always result in a predictable loss of concentration, the player has to change the way they respond. Remember, we choose our thoughts, so the player who constantly argues with a referee *chooses* to keep arguing, rather than taking the professional steps of *choosing* to focus on reacting quickly from the free-kick and looking to get the ball back in possession as quickly as possible. Whether a referee is right or wrong, no amount of self-distracting pleading with the official will actually make them change their mind, so the player should redirect their energy into doing something that they are in control of.

As the examples in the chart show, it is players' reactions to events that cause distractions, not the events themselves. It's impossible to be emotion free in the pressure of a game, but if you've got a clear picture of what your roles and goals are for the game,

'You don't close yourself off from the pressure,' he said. 'When everything is going crazy around you, the nerves are attacking your confidence, so it's important to keep everything exactly the same. The routine gives you the confidence to do it.

'You can hear the crowd, too. People always tell you to shut it out, but I don't think you can. You just have to live with it, accept the fact that it's there and function as normally as you would if it wasn't there.

'At the last moment my mind is a blank. I have focused on where I want to hit the ball, I'm thinking about which part of the foot I want to hit it with, to make sure my non-kicking foot's in position and where my weight's going. It all comes together, but it has become second nature, almost subconscious.'

Which is probably how that other dead-ball specialist, David Beckham, the England football captain, would describe his own approach to taking free kicks. In an inspired piece of advertising, Adidas recently brought the two together for a day and left them to their own devices with a bag each of footballs and rugby balls. Not surprisingly, both seemed equally adept at the other's skills, Beckham teaching Wilkinson his curling free kick and Wilkinson returning the favour with his goalkicking.

The Times newspaper profiling Jonny Wilkinson

you can make sure you are channelling focus and energy into fulfilling those roles. Show your passion and commitment to the team by how concentrated you can be, not by how much you can argue a case or enter into irrelevant battles with the opposition.

DEVELOPING DEAD-BALL ROUTINES

Here's the sport psychologist's favourite topic in football! After years of listening to players talk about the pressures of penalty shoot-outs, we'll try to give you some practical advice on how to maximize concentration and confidence for those times when you need to remain cool, calm, collected and focused under pressure.

Star Quote . . .

You can actually see your shirt moving over your heart where your heart is beating . . . there's no way I stand there in a game and kick and I'm perfectly relaxed . . . my heart is thumping like mad. What allows you to kick in that state is mentally knowing that you're prepared, mentally being correct, knowing that your routine's good and physically having the repetitive training that you've done enabling you to drop back into a subconscious sort of second nature.

Jonny Wilkinson speaking on his 'The Perfect 10' DVD/video. Essential viewing for any performer wanting to fulfil potential.

Feel free to pooh-pooh the ideas, after you have *fully* tried them out, and then also write to us and explain how Jonny Wilkinson is able to be so incredibly consistent with drop-goals and conversions, and how golfers can maintain their driving, chipping and putting performance under the most intense pressure (yes, we know there's a goalkeeper, but if Jonny Wilkinson can manage to place a rugby ball pretty much wherever he wants it, there's no reason why footballers shouldn't be able to strike a round ball in such a way that they can put it into an area of the goal that almost takes the keeper out of the equation). David Beckham is the consummate player when it comes to free-kicks and we can learn a great deal from his approaches too – other than the fact he practises more than most players. Alan Shearer, too, is almost unerring with his penalty taking, and you can very clearly see that he conforms to the key components of

> Practising penalties is garbage. You stand up and take them if you fancy it on the night.
>
> **Mick McCarthy**, after Ireland had been knocked out of the 2002 World Cup by missing three of their five penalties (and one in the match).
>
> *The Daily Telegraph*, 17/6/02)

> You can't recreate the pressure of taking penalties in front of 60,000 or 70,000 people on the training ground.

the psychology behind executing closed, self-paced skills.

The wonderfully self-defeating belief expressed in the two quotes at the top of this page will be slowly unpicked through this section by showing you how to build a concentration routine that will effectively allow you to focus on a corner, free-kick or penalty whether you are on the training ground, playing in baking heat, on a soaked winter pitch, or in front of five people or 50,000 people.

Alan Shearer - his penalty routine incorporates each of the suggestions outlined in these pages. © EMPICS

Had we been journalists reporting on the last World Cup, opposite is what we'd have written in our weekly column about the typical approach to penalties!

Tiger Woods can't recreate the pressure of driving off the 18th tee holding a one-shot lead, needing a par to win a million dollar tournament. Equally, he can't recreate the pressure of needing to make a 6ft putt to close the same tournament out. Regardless of not being able to recreate the pressure, he still practises. Jonny Wilkinson can't recreate the pressure of needing to make a drop-goal off his right foot with 30 seconds of the 2003 World Cup Final remaining, but this didn't stop him practising. In the DVD 'Jonny Wilkinson – The Perfect 10', the psychology behind his excellence is clear, and it boils down to two key components:

1. A superb pre-kick routine that is practised daily which prepares mind and body to execute the skill with maximum focus and belief.
2. A practise ethic that results in Jonny being able to concentrate only on the specific skills of executing the kick, wherever he is, so that when he is in the game situation, his concentration skills allow him to feel as if he is on the training pitch, and not in the heat of a full-scale match.

Therefore, football players can take control of their focus for dead-ball situations in exactly the same way. The development of these routines is simple, but the development of consistently using them is harder work

The Cheltenham Gazette, June 2002

Don't pay the penalty of poor preparation

To all but the most cynical of sports fans it must have been blessed relief that the outcome of the 2002 World Cup final was not decided by penalties. The better side won on the day. Simple, straightforward, no debate. How different the headlines might have been had Germany sneaked an unlikely win as a miserable consequence of the infamous penalty shoot out. Undesirable as this consequence may have been, far fetched it most certainly was not... and herein lies the issue. The prospect of penalties acting as the deciding influence in a World Cup final is a very real possibility and yet we know little of how each team would have prepared for, and consequently performed in, this torturously entertaining spectacle. What we do know is that Sven Goran Eriksson did indeed take the precaution of doing what he could to prepare our gallant young (mostly!) pretenders for this eventuality. And from the ranks of the professional sport psychologist I wholeheartedly applaud him.

Allegedly, Eriksson did what Glenn Hoddle and Bobby Robson before him chose not to do. He chose to maximize the chances of his team's success in the potential penalty shoot out by... yes... practising for it. Of course he accepted that one can never recreate the emotion of the moment... of knowing that the hopes of a nation lie in the outcome of this single kick of the simplest piece of sporting equipment with several zillion armchair critics ready to heap equal lashings of outcome-dependent praise or abuse. But he was also wise enough to appreciate that you can take a good stab at recreating the situation. How? By getting the players to actually walk from the halfway line to the penalty spot - as they would in reality. By getting them to use visualization techniques to replicate the sounds of the crowd outside and the emotional feelings within. No it's not the real thing - of course it isn't. But it's the next best thing - and that is the point. Why else does David Beckham spend countless hours practising his 'bend it like' tricks? Why else does Jonny Wilkinson relentlessly work on perfecting his art of slotting the oval ball between the uprights? Why else do Olympic athletes seek different ways of re-creating the emotion of the impending 60 seconds (less in some cases) that will be the most important of their life? Why? Because we KNOW that the more you practise a skill the less likely it is to break down under pressure. Even if you're not practising it in 'exactly' the same conditions as you will be performing it. You are habitualising a set of performance-related routines so that the execution of the skill is as robust as it can be. This is first year sport psychology material and Sven, once again, got it right.

When Mick McCarthy, so successful in most other aspects of his coaching duties, stated 'Practising penalties is garbage. You stand up and take them if you fancy it on the night' I am afraid I disagree - unpopular as this view may be in the light of how well the Irish team did after the departure of their volatile superstar Roy Keane. McCarthy's view simply does not stand up to scrutiny. It is too steeped in conventional football rhetoric. Thankfully, Eriksson is far removed from conventional football rhetoric and hence he presents a breath of fresh air in the often clichéd world of professional football. So show me the evidence of Sven's approach I hear you clamour. Witness David Beckham's penalty against Argentina. No it was not the greatest penalty ever seen. No it was not placed exactly where he would have liked. But boy was it struck with conviction and authority. Witness also his pre-kick routine. Slow, considered and purposeful. Plenty of deep breaths. Plenty of focusing and no doubt, plenty of visualization. These 30 seconds of video footage will be used in sport psychology classes for the next five years as much as Chris Waddle's miss in 1990 was used for opposite reasons.

In the sport psychology books you'll read about 3 distinct phases in this type of sports skill – physical set-up, mental set-up, and execution. Beckham got all three right under the most intense external and internal pressure. And that is why he is a great international sportsman... and why Eriksson is a great international coach.

Beckham probably will miss penalties in the future but it will not be because he hasn't practised or isn't focused.

Practice may not make perfect but at least it gives you a fighting chance.

Postscript – 2004

Despite missing two penalties in Euro 2004, Beckham remained, and remains, confident in himself and his routine. He was reported in The Daily Telegraph *(5/7/04) to have said 'If there's another penalty, I'll step up and take it. If I miss that, I'll step up and take another one ... I can look in the mirror and believe I've done my best.'*

although essential if players are going to be in the situation where they control the stress and tension of a penalty shoot-out, and it does not control them. The secret is, the player practises controlling thinking (what they focus on with their eyes and what thoughts they concentrate on), so they can switch into controlled thinking mode under any amount of pressure, and simply focus upon executing the skill.

The concentration routines we recommend have three key phases. These are:

Phase 1 – The Physical Set-up

Phase 2 – The Mental Set-up

Phase 3 – The Execution.

We'll now go through each of these steps and outline how you monitor and develop the

Example Content

Physical Set-up

- Place ball on spot with logo just below middle, centre of the ball.
- Take 4 steps back, and 1 to the side.
- Clean bottom of boots.
- Deep, relaxing breath and stand in balanced, centred stance.

Mental Set-up

- Focus eyes onto the logo.
- Visualize a line from the ball into the selected spot in the goal.
- Visualize striking the ball sweetly and powerfully, and the ball travelling along the path selected.
- Focus eyes back onto the logo.
- Deep breath, think 'balance and power'.
- Repeat cue word 'Shearer'.

Execution

- Take the penalty.
- Drive the ball along the visualized line with conviction. Driving foot through the logo.
- Strong follow-through, maintaining balance and power through the ball.

effectiveness of the routine to really help seal belief ready for use in match situations.

The specific details in the example are only used to show the simple focus on processes – the example *is not the way* to structure a routine, but it contains come useful pointers. There is clearly a *relaxation/calming component* that is used to get the body into the right state each time – it is important to be able to get the body into the right state of control – a player needs to be able to create this state whether they have just been hanging around for ten minutes waiting for their turn in the penalty shoot-out, or whether they have just sprinted two-thirds of the pitch before being fouled in the area.

There is also a focusing component – fixing the eyes in a consistent way so that the same visual information is being taken in each time. Keeping the eyes consistent in their physical focus is very important in helping keep the mind concentrated in the same way. Players need to experiment with the control of their eyes that works for them. There is no hard-and-fast rule as to how narrow or broad that focus should be, other than that it should be consistent. Most importantly, the eyes focus onto a familiar cue, and it becomes that much easier to block out everything else that is not critical to striking the ball.

Next is the visualization component. This is critical as it clearly gets the player focused on the process they want to go through – the quality of strike, and the path of the ball – these two things are totally in the control of the player. Get these right, and the keeper will have to make a great save to deny a goal. The player is really *controlling their controllables* here, and not worrying about missing, but focusing upon getting the processes right that give the best chance of success. The visualization gives a clear path to follow, and really pre-programmes the brain with very clear instructions to follow. Without the clear instructions, it is possible that a half-hearted penalty will be struck because a clear decision hasn't been made.

The final focusing component is the self-talk that in the example is concentrated upon technical checks and modelling of body language. The 'Shearer' cue word simply reminds the player to hit with power and conviction. The structured self-talk plays an important part in the tempo of the kick, so regardless of when the referee blows the whistle, the player is still finishing off the final elements of the routine at their own pace. We would definitely recommend practising the routine in training with a referees whistle being blown at various points in the routine, so that the player gets used to taking the kick at their own pace, rather than being put off by the whistle being blown at irregular points in the routine.

Monitoring and Evaluating the Routines.

Something we use a lot with the development of these concentration routines is a very simple format to keep track of how well the process is developing. You can use the scoring sheet we've provided overleaf to learn about how each critical step of performance is impacting upon scoring. We'd suggest doing the practices to begin with without a goalkeeper so you can really build up confidence in the processes of the routine. After the processes are really well in place, the goalkeeper can be reintroduced, and the scoring sheet continued with. Once the keeper is back in place the aim for the player would be to try to keep the scores on the scoring sheet as consistent as they had become without the keeper in place.

With the scoring sheet, after each simulated attempt (free-kick or penalty) you need to get a score for how well you managed to carry out the routine. Even though the elements are relatively simple, having the mental discipline to carry out each piece is hard work. Therefore, we would not expect players to execute the mental components of the routine perfectly each time. It will take a considerable amount of practice for players to get to the

Attempt	% Quality of Routine	% Quality of Strike	Path of Ball on Target (y/n)	Outcome
1				
2				
3				
4				
5				
6				
7				
8				
9				
10				
Average				

point where the quality of the visualization, relaxation and self-talk is perfect every time, so do make sure that you get feedback on this element of the routine. Next, rate the quality of the ball strike and whether the ball travelled along the chosen path that was visualized. Finally, when a goalkeeper is introduced, record the most important piece of information – whether a goal was scored!

You should notice that when the routine score is higher, ball strike rating will be higher, and providing that technique is good, the ball will follow the selected path and result in a goal (or at least force the goalkeeper to make a great save). As Jonny Wilkinson says, setting up a kick of any sort can become as accurate as firing a gun at a target – if you get the routine right and you have excellent technique from good practice, then the ball can't do anything but go where you want it to.

> I've always tried to have a professional attitude to training. I love it almost as much as I love playing.
>
> **David Beckham**
>
> (*David Beckham: My Side*, 2003)

Alan Shearer is great to watch for his consistent approach to taking penalties, and David Beckham the same for free-kicks around the area. Even though we see great consistency outwardly in what they do, they are also very likely to have great consistency mentally . . . and this is the key to great concentration.

Consistency in preparation maximizes the chance of consistency in performance!

STEP 5

Dealing with Pressure: Get Your Bottle Here

England debutant Glen Johnson admits he was suffering with huge nerves when he realized he was actually going to play for his country for the first time. The 19-year-old defender started on the England bench in their friendly against Denmark at Old Trafford, but had to come on sooner than expected when Gary Neville was forced off with an injury. The Chelsea right back says that he was struck down with nerves when he realized he was going to get on, but says that he hopes to get better with age and experience.

*'In the dressing room, I sat down and thought about what was actually happening and thought 'Oh s**t'*, said Johnson.

But once I got out there, I relaxed. I will get better with age and experience, like everyone else.
www.skysports.com (17/11/2003)

Footballers are very helful at providing us with quotes to bring alive some of the points we are making in these chapters. Predictably by now, you know that we're going to say that it's great that Glen Johnson knows he's going to get better with age and experience at managing his nerves, but rather than be like everyone else, we'd recommend that he does more than just wait for experience, and examine in detail some of the simple ideas that can help him take control of his nerves *now*. This section will provide simple ideas for how this element of the game can really be managed effectively and how players can maximize bottle and minimize the negative impact of nerves on performance.

Stress, nerves and sport go hand in hand. It's ironic that so much time is spent preparing for matches, and then, on match day, nerves can kick in and muck everything up. We know that a certain amount of stress and pressure is probably a good thing for most players. However, too much stress can have a negative impact, and without an ability to manage excessive levels of nerves, players will repeatedly 'bottle it' on big match days. Everyone knows players who are great on the training pitch, but whose nerves block their ability to rise to the occasion on Saturday at 3.00pm! If only the competitive matches could be played on the training ground . . . then everyone could see what a great player they are. Such

The greater our fear of making a mistake, the greater the likelihood that we will make a mistake.
Sven-Goran Eriksson
(*Sven-Goran Erikkson on Football*, 2002)

examples just go to show the impact of stress and nerves, and highlight how important it is to make sure that players take control of the stress and make sure that it is always working for them, rather than undermining them. In order to help understand how these kind of situations come about, there's some useful background information we can introduce you to.

> The Dutch are the hot favourites but Vogts insisted his players, who have not qualified for a major tournament since the 1998 World Cup, were not nervous. He said: 'Nerves? No, why? That is a footballer's life. All my players have to play maybe the best match of their lives and that is great.'
>
> www.football365.com

UNDERSTANDING STRESS, NERVES AND ANXIETY

If we think a player is not managing performance nerves very well, there's some important extra detail that needs uncovering. Players typically get nervous in two main ways. The most obvious nerves are the ones we feel within the body. We can all associate with at least one of the typical physical elements of nerves – butterflies, feeling tense, yawning, feeling nauseous, and increased heart rate and breathing. You can see extreme cases of these pre-match feelings sometimes when players will actually vomit before a match. Typically, though, players will have exactly the reaction that Glen Johnson reported 'But once I got out there, I relaxed'. The physical nerves usually disappear as soon as the player gets on to the pitch for the warm-up or when the whistle blows. The physical nerves have usually got progressively more intense in the build-up to the game. However, these nerves are not detrimental to performance on their own, and it is important for players to become aware of what the relationship is for them between the level of these nerves and how they play. It can be helpful to use the graph below to work out the impact of physical nerves on

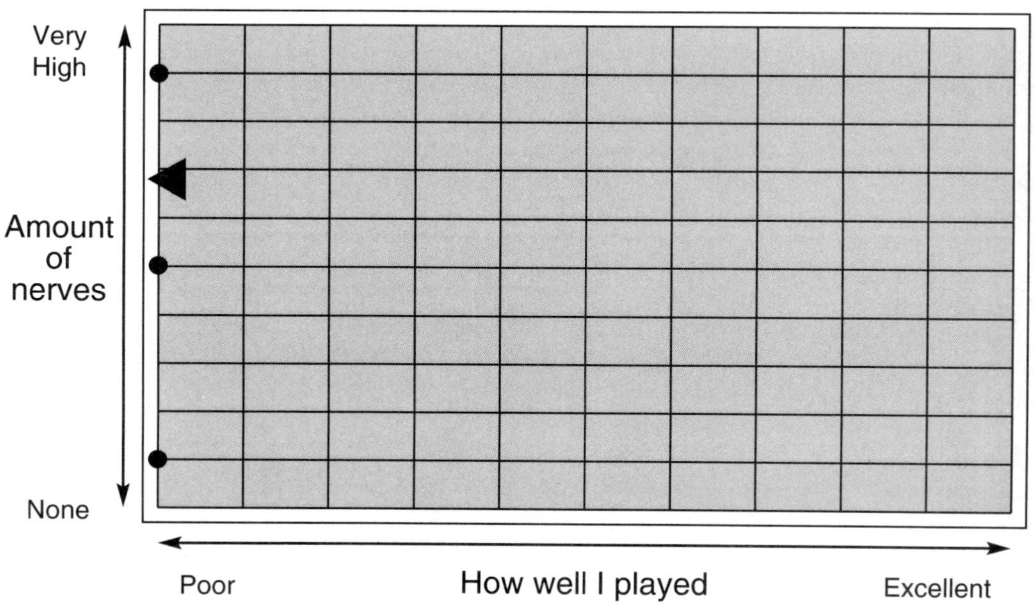

performance for you. Simply identify two different occasions when you experienced low, medium and very high amounts of physical nerves.

Having identified two different matches for each level of nerves, starting at the relevant dot, move along the 'how well I played' line and make a mark on the graph at the level that indicates how well you played. Do this until you have all six matches marked on the graph. It's possible that the marks won't be grouped quite as neatly as the example shown below, but whatever your grouping, you should be able to get a good feel for the relationship between nerves and performance. From the example below, we know there must be a level of nerves that equates with excellent performance, so we can predict that this is most likely to be when the player has a moderate to high level of nerves. Too few nerves, and it seems the player does not play well, and too many nerves and performance has dropped off also. This is probably the most typical kind of pattern, but we would certainly not expect to see this kind of pattern with every player.

It's critical that you spend time figuring out your 'Ideal Performance State' so that you can actually do something about it when you're outside the zone.

When performance is at the excellent level, we know that the level of nerves is exactly where it needs to be, and this is where the term 'in the zone' really comes from. For every player has their own 'zone', and even though the real 'peak performance' matches seldom happen in a career (where the player is almost playing on autopilot, feeling totally in control and invincible), it is possible to aim to get in your own zone as often as possible, which in turn maximizes the chances of you having those unbelievable days.

Because personal zones differ, there is always great individual variation in the charts. For example, you might find that very high levels of nerves and very few nerves, both lead to excellent performances (pretty much the opposite of the pattern shown). Equally, it might be that the more nerves a player feels, the better they notice they play. There are no rights or wrongs here. The important thing is

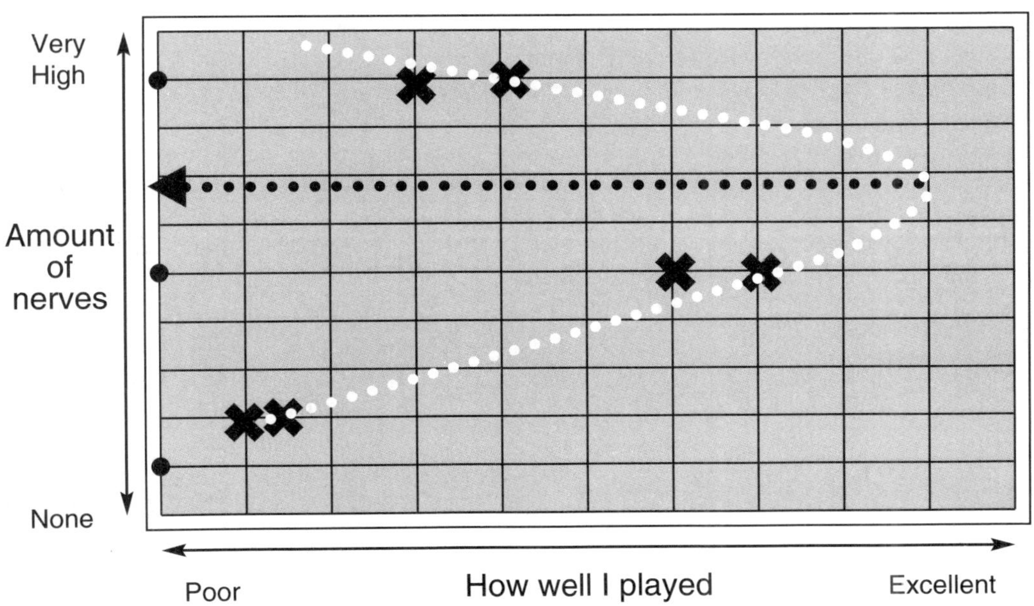

> I get so nervous before kick-off. All I want is for someone to come along from two hours in the future and say: 'It's fine. You played fine. Your team was great. No one got hurt.' I want the reassurance. But that person doesn't come. He never comes. And I'm left on the pitch not knowing what will happen.
>
> **Jonny Wilkinson**
> (*The Times*, 15/2/03)

> The most important thing for us to do is keep our heads as cool as possible . . . You don't need motivation in a game like this, everyone knows what is at stake. The players need motivating sometimes if you are playing less famous teams at home, but this is the biggest challenge since we played Germany away two years ago. I think it will be very tense, I'm sure we'll have a very dramatic 90 minutes, **and controlling nerves will be fundamental.**
>
> **Sven-Goran Eriksson**

to start to become aware of what the pattern is for individual players, so they can make sure they manage the amount of physical nerves they experience, in order to *give the best chance of producing a good performance*. We'll be going into detail about how to manage the nerves later in the chapter, but to begin with you have started to get a better feel for how nerves and performance work together.

The second kind of nerves that are experienced come directly from what is going on in our mind in the lead-up to a match. You might want to think of this as 'worry' rather than the very physical sensation of butterflies. Worry is made up of negative images and negative self-talk. Players might focus on pictures of playing poorly, or be concerned with thoughts about not performing well in front of a home crowd or against a specific opponent. You might also experience a player seemingly losing confidence in the lead up to the game – this is not usually lack of confidence, but is normally a result of the player *dwelling* on questions such as 'Will I be good enough?', 'Will I be subbed again?', 'Will I play well enough to impress that scout?', 'Will we win?', and so on. The player is so focused on the questions, that they don't focus on any potential solutions. Jonny Wilkinson's quote (above left) gives a really insightful perspective on the role of negative thoughts in the lead up to a game, and fortunately he is able to do something about these negative thoughts through his meticulous preparation in the lead-up to matches. If a player does not combat the negative thinking effectively then they usually get the physical nerves combining with the negative thinking, and this will not be helpful for these players when performing.

You might want to think of yourself in one of three ways and see which way best describes the role of worry for you in the lead up to a match:

1. As the match gets closer thoughts and images become increasingly negative. You notice that these thoughts are occurring more regularly and you don't seem to be able to put a stop to them. You don't enjoy having the thoughts and would prefer not to get this way prior to playing. It's possible that you worry about feeling nervous! Worrying about worry! The nerves you feel are certainly not helpful.

> Remember the old saying . . .
> *Butterflies are not a problem as long as you get them to fly in formation.*

> I've lived through many terrible things in my life, some of which actually happened.
>
> **Mark Twain**

2. You have a number of negative thoughts and images in the lead-up to a match. These grow in frequency as the match draws closer, but increasingly you use them as a cue to focus on how you are going to play so as to give yourself the best chance of getting the performance and result that you are seeking. The worry serves to make you take positive action – although the nerves don't feel great, you manage to overcome them and focus on more positive emotions.

3. You don't get particularly worried in the lead-up to a match. Your thoughts are primarily focused on the specific job at hand and how you will go about doing this to the best of your ability given the specific challenges of this game. Any nerves you do feel merely act to let you know that you are up for the game, and you'd interpret this feeling as positive rather than negative – that is, anticipation and excitement. You are probably more aware of other emotions as you prepare for the game rather than being focused upon just nerves.

Is there one of these three that describes you? You might want to fill in the pre-match thoughts and feelings chart that we've provided to help you make your decision, and perhaps see if you have your own category.

You'll see in Step 7 how important it is that you can begin to work out how you need to think and feel in the lead up to a match so that you can start to get into your Ideal Performance State each time that you play.

7 Steps Pre-match Feelings Chart **Date:**

The kind of thoughts I typically have in the few hours before a match are . . .

•
•
•

The kind of feelings I typically have in the few hours before a match are . . .

•
•
•

I think the *thoughts* I tend to have are *helpful/unhelpful* (delete as appropriate)

I think the *feelings* I tend to have are *helpful/unhelpful* (delete as appropriate)

I would ideally like to be *thinking and feeling* . . .

•
•
•

I can help to create these *thoughts and feelings* by . . .
Remembering how I felt before I played ________________
Saying ____ to myself every time I get a negative thought or feeling.
Reminding myself how ________________________________ (my role models) would be feeling and thinking before they played.

Typical worries of players that can cause negative thoughts

DEMAND WORRIES (The specifics of the challenge to be faced)

'This is a really intimidating ground to play at – the fans are so close to the pitch'.

'This team's unbeaten so far this season and on a roll'.

'This forward line we're playing against today can't stop scoring this season, and they're all so quick'.

'This surface is too dangerous for anyone to play on'.

ABILITY WORRIES (Do we or I have the skills or experience to cope?)

'This is the biggest crowd I've played in front of, I hope I don't choke'.

'There's no way we have the speed to cope with their forward line'.

'I just can't seem to play on these wet pitches'.

CONSEQUENCE WORRIES (What you think might happen if things go wrong)

'If I have another average game today I know I'm going to be subbed and probably dropped'.

'The boss is going to go ballistic again if we don't get a result today'.

'I could really get badly injured on this surface today'.

Since losing the 1976 final to Czechoslovakia we have never been defeated on penalties. We beat France 5-4 at the 1982 World Cup, and Mexico 4-1 four years later. We beat the English 4-3 in 1990 in Italy, and now 6-5 at Wembley. Notice the number of maximums. It is rare for German players to miss. The reason: we have the best nerves in the world.

Franz Beckenbauer
(*The Observer*, 30/6/96)

Coping self-talk to reduce negative thoughts

DEMAND WORRIES

'I've prepared really well this week, and it's a good test to see how well I can play with the fans so close to the pitch'.

'All good runs come to an end – it would be great to be the team that beats them first'.

'We've practised well this week on how to disrupt them, now we have to put the plan into action as effectively as we can'.

'Keep it simple, don't be flash, do the basics well and let the ball do the work on the surface'.

ABILITY WORRIES

'If I'm going to play at the highest level, they will be bigger crowds than this, so this is great practice for me'.

'We're great at reading the game in our back four, so we'll make sure that strength is used to counter their speed'.

'I can't get the pitch dried out, so I'll take on the challenge'.

CONSEQUENCE WORRIES

'Forget what might happen . . . stay in the present and play your best . . . relax and enjoy'

'Worrying about the boss is not helping me play well . . . so focus on doing your job well'

'You've got through matches like this on worse surfaces, so you'll manage it again'

It is hard to find the right words, but I will try. It is a game, was a game and will always be a game. We have not lost a battle, nor a war; nobody has lost their lives. We have lost a game.

Franz Beckenbauer
(www.manchester.com)

Whether you're coming on from the bench, or in the starting eleven, you'll need to make sure you can take control of your nerves and get them working for you as positively as possible.

It's also worth reading through the typical kind of worries that players experience before a match to help you become more aware of the kind of things that might be leading to negative thoughts. You can use these examples to help you decide what causes you the most concern.

If you feel you have a tendency to think excessively about any of these three kinds of worry then you can use the self-talk idea presented in Step 2 to decide how you want to shift from these statements to a more helpful focus. You can see the next table to show how easy it is to move from a negative, unhelpful thought, to a more positive and helpful statement. Once again, it's better to take control of this thinking and at least know that you gave yourself the best chance of performing well by thinking in a way that is designed to help you rather than get in your own way.

You'll have picked up from the previous sections and in the chart that being nervous is not always a bad thing, and some players definitely need the nerves in order to play well. We know from talking to hundreds of performers from many different sports that the trick with pre-performance nerves is actually a question of interpretation . . . *do you interpret your pre-match nerves as a good thing or a bad thing?* If you think that the nerves are bad and unhelpful, then chances are, they will be bad and unhelpful! If you decide that it's natural that you feel nerves in the lead-up to a game, and that they are simply a sign of your mind and body getting you ready to face the challenges of the 90 minutes, then the nerves

CHANGING HOW YOU THINK ABOUT NERVES

UNHELPFUL	HELPFUL
'****!! I'm so nervous, I can't believe how I'm feeling'.	'The nerves mean I'm really up for this match . . . great!'.
'These butterflies just aren't going away – I feel so uncomfortable'.	'This is just part of the build-up . . . it doesn't mean I'll play badly, and they'll go as soon as the whistle blows'.
'Feeling like this can't be good, I'll never play well'.	'Most people feel like this . . . I bet I can handle it better than them'.
'The time is going so slowly . . . this pressure just seems to be lasting for hours'.	'I'll take control of the time and use it effectively . . . I'll do some visualization to focus me on the game'.
'I've got so much nervous energy, I can't sit still'.	'This energy is really building up ready for kick-off . . . I'll channel it and use it to my advantage.'.
'I feel so tired with these nerves . . . I can't stop yawning'.	'You know this always happens with important games . . . don't worry about it and stick to the routine.'

> Once the whistle's gone those nerves are redirected. You're reacting to what's going on in the field. You just have to trust your ability and your preparation. That's the bit I like. But it's a real crunch situation.'
>
> **Jonny Wilkinson**
> (www.scrum.com)

will be a welcome part of the build-up. For some players it's easy to get them to change their beliefs about nerves, but for others a different tack might have to be taken as you'll see later in this section. So, rather than trying to get rid of nerves altogether to begin with, see if using the ideas in the table can help you get a positive spin on feeling the natural nerves that are part and parcel of playing. You can use Step 7 to help you be prepared for how you're going to feel at different stages in the build-up to a game. Once you know this, you can then decide what you're going to think and how you're going to make these feelings work for you. You can use the table we've provided to help you work through reframing some of your pre-match nerves.

MANAGING NERVES DIRECTLY

Although we'd advocate making sure you get your pre-match nerves to work for you, there are times when you need to take nerves on, head-on. No matter how much of a positive spin you put on the nerves, at the end of the day they are disruptive to performance, so have to be reduced. If this is the case, we'd actually recommend seeking out a sport psychologist to provide you with a tailored nerve-management plan. However, there are a

TAKING CONTROL OF PRE-MATCH NERVES
Making sure you have a positive spin!

Point in build up to the game	How I normally think/feel	Remember
Waking up.	Really feel the nerves kick in . . . a bit of apprehension	I've felt like this since I started playing . . . it's part of the build-up.
Getting to the ground.	Feel heart rate increases . . . makes me feel panicky	This isn't panic, just adrenalin – the day you don't get this you should worry!
Seeing the opposition warming up.	Start thinking about how good they look, how quick/skilful, etc.	This is helping you get ready for the match – don't worry about them, just control the quality of your own warm-up.
Kick-off.	All nerves drain away!	This always happens, so there's no need to worry excessively about any nerves before now! They have been helping you.

couple of things that you can try that might allow you to get greater control over your nerves, and lessen the impact of them upon your performances.

Whichever you think might work for you we'll give you no more important advice than the fact that you *must* practise these techniques regularly if they are ultimately going to be effective for you. There's no point thinking they will be a quick-fix. If you really want to eradicate nerves from your game, then you have to practise hard at nerve control techniques, just as you would with any other skill that you want to be able to use in the match context . . . so, give yourself a training regime and see how well you can stick to it. The thing that separates the great players from the also-rans is that they stick with the things they need to over time. They put knowledge into action, rather than just thinking it's sufficient to know what they should be doing – and when they really need it, that's when they'll get around to making the necessary changes.

THE 7-SECOND CONTROL PLAN

You'll see plans like this in many sport psychology books. It's simple to practise, has only three parts and can be useful for you both pre-match and in-match. And . . . it only takes 7 seconds!!

Part 1 involves making a physical change in how you're moving . . . *slow down*. So, in the lead up to the match, make sure you are not rushing around, letting nervous energy get the better of you. If you walk slowly, talk slowly, and just adjust your thinking speed, you'll be making sure that the current situation is not controlling you . . . you'll be controlling it.

TAKING CONTROL OF PRE-MATCH NERVES **Making sure you have a positive spin!**		
Point in build up to the game	**How I normally think/feel**	**Remember**
•	•	•
•	•	•
•	•	•
•	•	•
•	•	•
•	•	•

Interestingly, when we feel very nervous, we usually do things at a much quicker pace than we normally would, so by slowing down, you'll be getting back to a normal speed, even though you might feel like you're moving in slow motion.

Part 2 involves you taking even more control over how you're feeling by simply focusing on taking a couple of deep breaths – control your breathing to get in control of your body. Make sure these breaths come from the stomach, and fully inhale and exhale . . . the breaths should be controlled and should help to relax the upper body.

Part 3 simply involves you getting your *focus* back to the hear and now. Get your concentration back onto something that you're immediately in control of and this helps give you a sense of being in charge. Therefore, if it's before the match, just focus on the next small bit of preparation you have to do. If you're in a match situation, give yourself a positive focus onto something that you're totally in control of – good first touch, simple pass, strength in the tackle, whatever is a useful cue to remind you that you can do the simple things very well, and once again, you're in control of your actions and reactions.

Make sure you develop your ability to use the 7-second cure during training sessions. The more confident you feel that you are able to make it work in training, the easier it will be for you to use it automatically in match situations.

This technique is so simple, it would be easy to dismiss it. However, get the simplicity of it working for you and take control of your nerves. And don't forget – good sport psychology is often a set of common-sense principles that don't get applied at the critical moments!

7-Second Control Plan

1. SLOW DOWN : walk and talk
2. BREATHS : controlled and full
3. THOUGHTS – FOCUS : simple and NOW.

Focused Breathing Routines

If you feel you need more work on gaining control over the physical side of your nerves, then you might need to practise a more structured breathing technique. Many of the relaxation techniques that are used in everyday life revolve around using controlled breathing to regain control of the body, and remove

Five Steps to Controlled Breathing

Step 1: Find a place where you can sit down and will not be disturbed (most athletes find a toilet cubicle ideal for this!)
Step 2: Breathe deeply in through the nose and out through the mouth according to the following routine and while you are doing this, focus on relaxing your arms and shoulders.

Inhale through the nose: Count *in*, two, three, four.

Exhale through the mouth: Count *out*, two, three, four.

Step 3: Breathe deeply in through the nose and out through the mouth according to the same routine but this time focus on relaxing your legs and feet.

Inhale through the nose: Count *in*, two, three, four

Exhale through the mouth: Count *out*, two, three, four.

Step 4: Repeat this breathing process as many times as you are able, or as many times as you need.
Step 5: Stand up and silently repeat 'I feel ready – I feel in control.'

10 Steps to Deep Relaxation

Step 1: Find a place where you can lie down or sit down comfortably with your head supported in some way.
Step 2: Put on some music that you find really relaxing. Your personal CD player will be a great help here.
Step 3: Close your eyes and then spend a couple of minutes getting really comfortable and tuning in to your body.
Step 4: Now focus on your breathing rhythm. Take ten deep breaths to establish a slow steady breathing rhythm. Each time you breathe out, feel more relaxed and feel some tension begin to disappear.
Step 5: When you feel ready, focus on your right arm. Clench your fist tightly, count to ten, and then slowly open out your fingers and relax your hand completely. Feel your arm go heavy and sink towards the floor. Repeat this process once. Then run through the same process for your left arm.
Step 6: Now focus on your right leg. Tighten the muscles in your leg, count to ten and then relax all the muscles completely. Feel your leg go heavy and sink towards the floor again. Then run through the same process for your left leg.
Step 7: Turn your attention to your face, neck and shoulders. Relax all the muscles in this area and, in particular, focus on smoothing out the muscles in your forehead. Relax your cheeks, your neck and the back of your shoulders.
Step 8: Focus on relaxing your whole body by concentrating on a relaxed feeling in your finger-tips, toes, and forehead.
Step 9: Spend several minutes listening to your music, enjoying this relaxed feeling and imagining yourself in a place where you can feel completely relaxed and at ease. This may be on the beach, by a swimming pool, or in a forest.
Step 10: Count down silently, and slowly from 10 to 1. As you do so, bend and stretch your arms, move your head from side to side and gradually bring yourself back to full alertness with your eyes open. As you get to number 1 you should feel fully relaxed, rested, refreshed and *in control.*

many of the uncomfortable symptoms in the body that are associated with being under pressure. We've given you 5- and 10- step routines here that will allow you to develop your ability to get control over your body.

You should find in time that these routines will allow you to get a great sense of control over your body, and get you to a level of readiness that is ideal for you. If you like, you can use these techniques to get you fully relaxed, before you perhaps go through your normal warm-up routine that will get your body to the correct level arousal for beginning the game. It's often easier to slowly increase the level of adrenalin through a warm-up rather than constantly trying to calm yourself down. As well as using the physicality of a normal warm-up to bring your arousal levels up to the right intensity before the game, you might want to consider building in some other techniques that can help you get 'psyched-up' once you are in control of your nerves.

Psyching Up!

Once players are in control of their nerves, it is obviously important that they are mentally and physically warmed up and ready to play once the whistle goes. You don't want to be so relaxed still that you are not actually up to speed for the game. You might consider using one of the following to help you make sure that you are switched on to the right level and ready to play.

Use Inspirational Music
Just as with the relaxation exercise, music can help you get pumped up ready to play. The choice of music is obviously very personal, but you want to make sure that whatever you choose has a positive emotional impact on you. You want the music to get you feeling positive, pumped up and ready to play. Many of the highlights montages on TV use great motivational music, so you could start to pay attention to these to get some clues as to what might work for you. Once you have your selection, keep it in your kit-bag and use it as part of your preparation as and when you need it. The music can often help to block out other distractions thus allowing you to focus on your thoughts for the match.

> There are three types of inspirational music that sport performers use – 1. Sporting connection music such as *Chariots of Fire* or *Rocky*; 2. Patriotic music like anthems and nationalistic songs; 3. Meaningful lyrics like Tina Turner's *Simply the Best*, M People's *Proud* or Queen's *We Are the Champions.*

The Physical warm-up
Obviously, all teams warm up before a game, and this physical warm-up has a great impact on levels of arousal and readiness. Therefore, make sure that you are using this time to get maximum psychological benefit as well as getting the muscles primed for performance, and the heart and lungs ready to play. The physical changes obviously have an impact on how you're thinking, so make sure that you factor this in to your pre-match routine to get you into your 'zone'.

Activating Reminders
Some players actually love the pressure and thrive on the build-up to the match. It is very easy for these players still to make changes to their state of readiness by using some reminders that give an extra charge to the preparation. Strong, positive statements shouted aloud, or spoken with passion internally can really help to get arousal level to the area it needs to be, and give an extra boost just prior to the action beginning, or at the resumption of the second half.

You can come up with your own mantra that give you the final spur as you leave the dressing room . . . but here are some we've heard used to good effect in the past.

'We're here to do the testing . . . not to be tested!'

'Let's do it – dominate from the first tackle!'

'No prisoners . . . we're in charge!'

'Let's make them more scared of us than we are of them!'

'Total commitment – 90 minutes to prove ourselves.'

Although these are being shouted by one player to team-mates, it's likely that they are really positive reminders for the player shouting them out. Consider what you can say that will have maximum impact for you and for the players around you.

AND FINALLY . . . . ENJOY THE CHALLENGE!

Pressure is part and parcel of competitive sport. If you can't deal with it, you are always going to struggle to achieve your best on the big day. We've tried to give you a variety of tips and tricks in this section to help you build up an individualized coping plan but don't forget just how important enjoyment is as part of that plan.

We encourage performers to enjoy the

'great white heat of competition'. We encourage them to enter the competition arena looking as if they are excited about the prospect of competing. Even when things aren't going so well, we encourage them to focus on enjoying the challenge of digging their way back. So our final message in this section is to start really enjoying the challenge of tough competition. Grit your teeth and hang in there all the way to the very end. Enjoy the whole process and compete with a determined smile on your face! We'll let David Beckham finish this section by his description of Sven-Goran Eriksson's final words to the England team prior to the famous 5–1 victory over Germany in the World Cup qualifying match in 2001.

> Sven sat everyone down. What he had to say was pretty simple but tapped into everybody's mood. 'Go out and enjoy yourselves. Be confident. They're a good team but we're a better team. Play well. And three points'.
>
> (*David Beckham: My Side*, 2003)

STEP 6:

Teamwork – United!!

> In my business, togetherness is not just a nice concept that you can take or leave according to taste. If you don't have it, you are nothing. Selfishness, factionalism, cliquishness are all death to a football team . . . As a manager in football, I have never been interested in simply sending out a collection of brilliant individuals. There is no substitute for talent but, on the field, talent without unity of purpose is a hopelessly devalued currency.
>
> **Sir Alex Ferguson**
> (In *The 90 Minute Manager*, 2002)

Despite football being a team sport, there are many fundamentals of 'united' psychology that get overlooked. Alex Ferguson's words cut to the very heart of the issue . . . 'talent without unity of purpose is a hopelessly devalued currency'. Developing a unity of purpose will be the main focus of this step. As an individual reading this book, you can make sure that within your team you are doing everything you can to ensure that you are playing your team role as well as performing to your peak individually. As a coach reading this book, you can ensure that the fundamentals of the team step are put into place with your squad.

We'd like to really challenge you to avoid simply *assuming* that you already do the things that we'll outline in this section. In our experience, these fundamentals can always be done better and indeed are often taken for granted and hence dealt with quite poorly. The processes we will outline take time to complete in team meetings, and will therefore not feature a ball very much. Talking time is usually devalued against training time, but we can guarantee that if you spend time getting the communication right within your team you'll get far more effective training time as a result.

We'll present the fundamentals in a logical sequence that allows the cohesion of the team to be established and strengthened. Team goal-setting is usually a good place to start.

TEAM GOALS – GETTING THE TEAM ON THE SAME PAGE

The first rule of team dynamics is to ensure that there is a clear, shared mission that the team is embarking on, that is unity of purpose. Therefore, as a team, it is essential that there is

> We always knew they were strong in terms of technique and movement but this year has shown their mental strength as well. Anybody who can come back from two goals down at Juventus and win is a mental giant. If they can keep their winning mentality for 90 minutes, they'll take home the European Cup.
>
> **Giovanni Trapattoni**
> (www.manchester.com)

Are You Really United?

Does every member of your team *share and believe in* the same vision of what the team/club is trying to achieve?

Do they know *and accept* 'why' goals and targets are in place?

Do they believe that these targets are realistic for the team?

Have the players been involved in helping to establish the 'what, why and how' for this team?

Does every member of the team have a clear picture of what improvements need to take place in order for the likelihood of success to be maximized?

Do they have a picture of how the team will be building towards success over time – short, medium and long-term aims?

David Beckham: Communication, I think, is the biggest thing and you've got to have a good communication with the players and with the coach and with the whole staff team.

Adapted from transcript from interview with David Frost on BBC *Breakfast with Frost*

a clear outlining of the Outcome, Performance and Process goals for the team as a whole, i.e., what we want to achieve, how we need to perform, what we need to focus on when performing (remember from Step 1). Without unity of purpose, the various physical, mental, technical and tactical resources that the team are individually and collectively in possession of do not get pooled and directed towards specific achievements. A team can still be effective without these goals, but inconsistency in performance is likely to be far greater, and the elusive team spirit is much more fragile. The more that the team share a vision of what it is trying to achieve, and how they need to go about achieving it together, the greater the collective drive becomes and we move towards the much-sought-after situation of 'the whole being greater than the sum of the parts'.

The processes that we'll outline take up time. Most businesses that we know who employ these procedures as a matter of course, due to them being an essential part of their success, devote considerable blocks of time to the process. Players and coaches might not be used to spending consolidated periods of time sitting down and talking about training and performing, but if you are really going to develop a united team, you have to invest the time. We obviously appreciate the importance of actual practice time, but during the course of an 8–10 month season, there is no reason why several days should not be devoted to the planning side of performance. So, we urge you to prioritize some quality talking time and factor in some meetings on your training programme. These meetings need to be seen as integral parts of the training programme, so make sure that they are presented to the players in exactly the same way as a fitness session or skills session would be. Equally, you would want to make sure that the players realize that you are looking for effort, commitment and contribution in these sessions in exactly the same way as you would on the training ground. Players would not be allowed to drift through a training session putting in minimum concentration and effort, and the same should be true for team meetings.

Visions and Missions . . . What Are You Really Trying to Achieve?

Most goal setting in football is forced into a very short-term, season at a time, time-frame. In terms of an overall vision for the team, you might want to think about setting a long-term target for what the club is trying to achieve. This might be a 3-5 year aim or longer if you

> As a group, these United boys have got a lot in common. They know everything about the club and understand the demands. They might have seen 100 games at Old Trafford before being asked to play one. None of their rivals have got that.
> **Kevin Keegan** (www.manchester.com)

choose. These visions help to develop a sense of perspective for players, and also create some targets that are about much more than just winning games of football. Players and staff alike can see how they would be contributing to the long-term success of the club, and not just short-term success. Once a vision is in place, the attitudes and values that you want to promote within the club to help with realizing the vision can be communicated. Decisions that are made, requests that are made, other targets that are set all start to become accountable to the vision; there is always a reason 'why' we need to do things this way, because this is 'how' it's helping us get closer to our final aim.

As you can see, it is possible to set your vision in a number of ways. You might choose to think about setting new standards and creating some new benchmarks. Equally, your team might be best served by using comparisons with existing successful teams, and throwing down the gauntlet to match these standards that have been shown elsewhere. If circumstances require it, you may want to set your vision so that it is deliberately confrontational, as in the final example. The different examples serve to bring about motivation in slightly different ways, and success can be interpreted differently depending upon the values of the club and those involved with it. Whatever your choice, these big picture targets can set the scene for longer-term success, and are an essential part of any successful team or organization.

You must be prepared to take some risks with your vision. Simply setting a vision that keeps everyone in their comfort zone will not take you to new levels. Feel free to set vision goals that keep everyone training and playing in a way that they are used to, but if you really want to make progress with your team, you have to start raising the bar to a level where people are thinking 'This vision is unreasonable isn't it?' Even though these thoughts are present, the kinds of teams that set these goals usually have an attitude that says 'Well, it

Example Team Visions

- By the end of the 2008 season, we will have set a new high standard for discipline and fair play that will be matched by our consistency in performances.
- In five seasons' time, we will have become the most effective defensive team in the history of the league, which will be our foundation for winning matches consistently.
- Over the next four years, we will become the most respected team in terms of our professionalism. We will be consistently the fittest, best prepared, tactically intelligent and most envied club in the league.
- By 2006, we are going to be the team that every other team wants to beat – we are going to become the Manchester United of our league and look forward to setting some new standards for excellence at this level.
- Our aim is to become the football equivalent of the England Rugby Team in terms of professionalism, performance and winning ability. We will develop a winning mindset that will take us to success at all levels of the club. This will be the focus on the first four years of our ten-year vision.
- Our purpose is to slowly but surely remove Harchester United from their position of dominance in this league. In three years' time, they will no longer be the best team around.

> Yes it's important to be proud when you put on your team shirt. In a winning culture, people think, 'We're good, we have nothing to be afraid of. We're not bothered by what the opposition do. We do our own thing.'
>
> **Sven-Goran Eriksson**
> (*Sven-Goran Erikkson on Football*, 2002)

might sound unreasonable, but we believe we can do it, and you can guarantee that if we don't try, someone else will, and we're not prepared to let someone else get there first.'

So, your vision really needs to be very clear and really provide a reason for your players to turn up to training and be involved in contributing to a great achievement. It will be very obvious when the vision has been fulfilled, and the vision in itself will be so clear that there is no room for not knowing what the vision is all about. The vision should be exciting and challenging and really get the competitive juices of the club flowing – everyone will be eager to be involved. The examples we've given could actually be made more daring, risky and bold. Consider a vision that states 'Our club is going to set the standards of professionalism and excellence in all British sport by the end of the decade – we will have other sports coming to us to find out what our secret of success is.' You need to decide upon the level of audacity that you want with your goals in relation to your team, your level of performance and the type of players you are dealing with. Without a great guiding vision, Wimbledon Football Club would not have achieved its rise from non-league football to FA Cup winners in such a short space of time. The relative downturn in Wimbledon's fortunes provides another important element of the vision. Critically, when we do achieve the vision, a new one must be set in order to keep the momentum of progress moving and everyone compelled to achieve some new equally exciting goals. Without a new vision the central desire and purpose of all involved disappears. Instead of aspiring to achieve some bold goals, it is possible that a team becomes focused on making sure that 'we don't fail'.

It's really important to ask the following five questions about a team vision:

- Does the vision generate a sense of forward momentum, change and progress for us as a team?
- Does the vision excite everyone and get them taking action?
- Does the vision unite us and help to create pride and passion in the team?
- Is the vision brash, bold and will it raise eyebrows?
- Does the vision mean we are going to create something that we will be proud to be associated with when it is consigned to history?

Our favourite guiding vision that we have seen work so effectively in sport is that of Steve Redgrave and Matthew Pinsent in their coxless pair and as part of the Sydney Gold Medal-winning coxless four with Tim Foster and James Cracknell. The overall goal that fuelled these truly professional athletes was to make sure that *'On our worst day, we are good enough to beat anybody else in the rest of the world.'* This is a truly bold goal. With such an aim to aspire to you can imagine how this philosophy influenced motivation, desire and commitment to every training or racing day through a year. This was a truly uniting vision that impacted on preparation and performance, and was certainly at the heart of their success along with their coach Jurgen Grobler. If you consider that training would consist of at least three sessions per day of 90 minutes, for six days a week, 48 weeks per year, you begin to realize why such a goal is needed in order to help produce daily quality that will result in ultimate confidence when sitting on the start line of an Olympic final. Four years of preparation to get six minutes of performing absolutely spot-on requires a powerful vision! If you mess up on this day, you don't have another game just around the corner to make up for it – you've just wasted four years'! There's no reason why a powerful vision can't be created to help football teams rise to the challenge of peaking regularly for important match after important match . . . you just have to have the imagination to set the vision!

FROM VISION TO ACTION

Once the big picture targets are in place you can focus more on the conventional goal-

A Team Goal-Setting Agenda for Coach/Manager
(Meeting time, 90 minutes minimum)

- Break the team up into small groups of 3–4, with a mix of positions and experience.
- Provide each small group with a sheet of flip-chart paper and pen.
- On a main flip-chart that all the groups can see, have the following question visible. *'What should we be aiming to achieve by the end of this season in terms of league position?'*
  - Dream end position
  - Challenging but realistic end position
  - Minimum position we should accept.
- Give the groups ten minutes or so to come up with their three answers. Make sure that they agree within the groups before they commit their answers to paper.
- Have each group come up to the flip-chart and write their answers on the master sheet, giving a brief explanation of why they have given their answers. This should take another 10–15 minutes.
- You will be able to use the results now on the board to have a wider discussion amongst the team with the aim of coming to a consensus target for each of the three goals. (The final, agreed targets need to be recorded for later use.)
- You now need to show another question to the groups. *'If we are going to achieve our finish position target what qualities will we repeatedly need to show on the pitch, game by game?'*
  - Tactical qualities
  - Fitness qualities
  - Mental qualities
  - Other.
- Each group should identify a maximum of five qualities in each area.
- Give the groups at least 15 minutes to come up with their responses to these questions. You may find you need longer as there is a lot to cover here. All the while, you must be encouraging the players to be thinking about the strengths they see in the team and using these to help come up with the qualities.
- The remainder of the session should be spent with the groups presenting their top qualities and giving a brief outline of why they think these are important. As you listen, note down all the qualities from each group under the headings. You should find that there are similar themes beginning to emerge that can be grouped together.
- Present the agreed goals back to the players on a personal goal sheet, and display the agreed goals in a prominent place at the training ground and in the home changing room.

setting that has typically taken place in sport. The scene has been set, and now it is essential to identify the specific things that need to be achieved in order to start bringing the vision closer to reality. Therefore, a considerable amount of time needs to be spent getting the team on the same page so that the resources of the team can be pooled and directed towards specific action in training and matches. As you carry out more and more of these goal-setting exercises, you'll really start to appreciate how effective they can be in developing unity and purpose.

We would always recommend that the team are actually involved in the goal-setting process rather than having the goals imposed upon them. It takes time for the team to get used to being involved in this process, but you will see how their involvement can actually be of great benefit to the development of accountability to each other within the team.

As we saw in Step 1 in the development of the winning mind, you have to make sure that the outcome, performance and process goals

Weir United FC 2004–5 Targets

Our team is united this season in the pursuit of . . .

- Our dream goal of a cup WIN and a top three finish in the league.
- Our challenging goal of a top five finish in the league.
- At the very least, a top six finish to improve on last year's finish place.
- Being the most improved team in the league this year and building a strong base for the next few seasons.

We are united in achieving our goals by:

- Focusing on winning 60% of our home games and 40% away from home.
- Making sure our game stats stay consistently good from match to match.
- Using our attacking talent to always outscore our opponents in the shots on target category and total attempts on goal category.
- Making sure we don't ever lose three games on the trot.

We will make sure that we will approach training and matches:

- With every player knowing what their role is and what is expected of them, every session, every match.
- Switched on, and focused on staying in the present.
- With total commitment to developing and exploiting our fitness to a new standard for us.
- With an attitude that makes sure we 'never say die' and maintain commitment and effort throughout training and matches.
- By always backing each other and helping each other to achieve new personal highs this year.
- With us valuing our communication both on and off the pitch.

We will review progress on this chart every 4–6 weeks through the season.

REMEMBER YOUR COMMITMENT TO OUR TEAM MOTTO

PERSONAL RESPONSIBILITY IN DELIVERING EXCELLENCE

are all in alignment. Therefore, when working on unity, you have to go through this process with the team. We would recommend using a series of team meetings to get all of the goal-setting organized for the team. During the course of the goal setting you might want to use the performance profiling exercise outlined within Step 1. This will fit in with the goal setting meeting agenda that we've supplied on page 108. When using the profiling and the goal-setting agenda, the final aim is to produce a final document that can be given to each player and also displayed for the team if appropriate.

We've provided a sample form that can be used for communicating the agreed goals to everyone, but you should experiment with the best way for you to get the message across to the team. You might wish to use more visual methods and develop your own images to show how the goals will link together.

TEAM PROFILING TO ESTABLISH AIMS AND PROCESSES

Within a team meeting, performance profiling is an excellent technique for improving communication and also making clear the challenge for improving as a team. We would use the following approach to get the most out of a profiling session with a team:

2004 Team Targets

Our team is united this season in the pursuit of . . .

-
-
-
-

We are united in achieving our goals by:

-
-
-
-

We will make sure that we will approach training and matches:

-
-
-
-
-
-

REMEMBER YOUR COMMITMENT TO OUR TEAM MOTTO

PERSONAL RESPONSIBILITY IN DELIVERING EXCELLENCE

1. In small groups have the players generate a list of words that describe the characteristics that a winning team possesses. The players should be encouraged to think of all possible characteristics.
2. Translate all of the individual characteristics onto a main list at the front of the meeting room. Make sure everyone understands what each of the characteristics means. Group the characteristics under the headings of TACTICAL, FITNESS, ATTITUDE and TEAMWORK (technical is usually covered in individual goal-setting)
3. Ask the players to look through the list and identify any of the characteristics that *should not* be applied to the targets set by this team. Cross off any characteristics where a consensus is reached that they are not wholly relevant.
4. The next element constantly needs to be related back to the question of 'What is our current level of achievement on this characteristic?'. If the team was already the finished article they would score 10 out of 10 on each characteristic. It is unlikely that they are the finished article on any quality, so get the small groups to go through the list and give a score for each quality.
5. Get the groups to come up to the main board and write their scores next to each quality. You will be able to see what the average score is for each quality.
6. From the average scores, get the team to decide which are the three most important characteristics that *need immediate development*, and which are the three most important characteristics to be earmarked for improvement over the course of the whole season. You should also make sure that the strengths of the team are highlighted – this is important for team confidence and a balanced perspective.
7. The final element of the meeting now

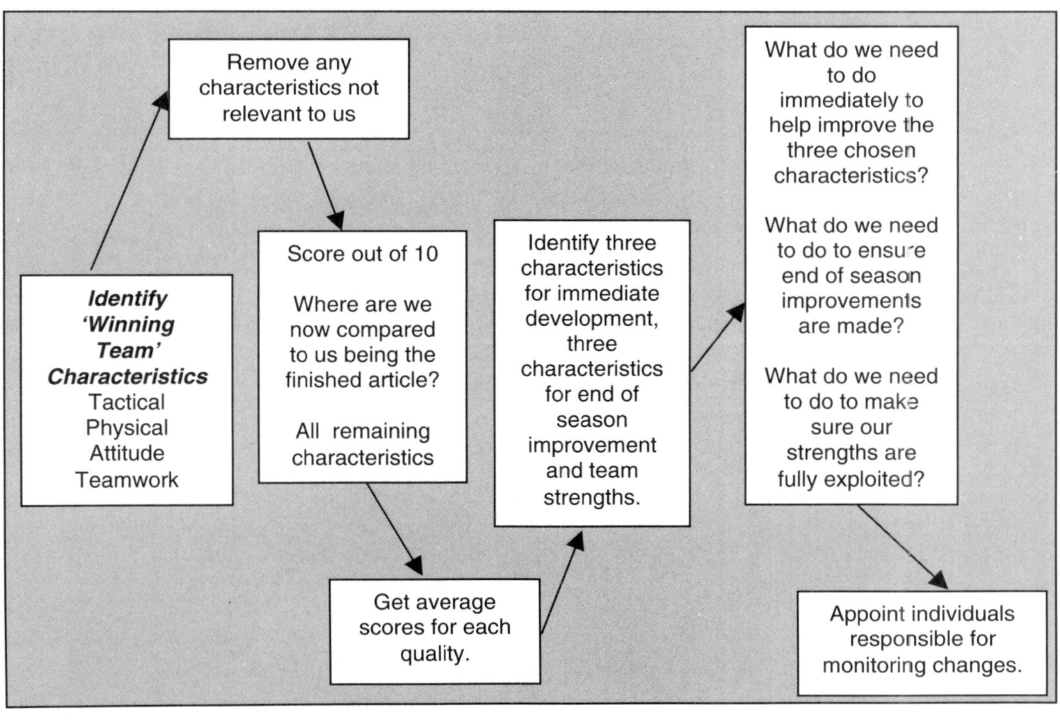

focuses upon what needs to actually be done if these areas are going to be improved upon. The team should decide upon some action to be taken *collectively* and *individually*. Therefore, every player has personal responsibility for making a difference, as well as knowing that the whole team is making an effort to improve. Points of action are decided upon for both the short term and longer term aims, and this is most effectively achieved by going through each item using the prefix of 'In order to improve our *(quality identified)*, we need to make sure that as a team we *(take some action)*'. Get the players to consider how they need to modify their thinking and adapt their behaviours in order to bring about the desired change.

8. Finally, as an option you can select a group of three or four players who will be responsible for helping monitor and implement the changes. Each player might be given a couple of areas for which they are responsible. In this way, you ensure that the players feel fully involved in the development of the team.

We've summarized this process in the form of a flow-chart (on page 113) to help you keep things as simple as possible.

Even if you don't go into elaborate detail to develop your goals as a team, the one thing that you must make sure happens is that there is a *shared acceptance* within the team of the goals. Shared goals are right at the very heart of team spirit or team cohesion, so you have to make sure that you have a group of players who are all focusing their efforts towards the same outcome. You can't do too much to ensure that all of your team are pulling in the same direction.

> Only a team player who has been involved in a major event can understand the sense of togetherness that sends the dressing-room temperature soaring in the moments before going out for the kick-off. It is an indescribable feeling, but you can almost reach out and touch it. It's a combination of harmony, brotherhood and a desire to do well not only for oneself but for each other. In short, it's team spirit.
>
> **George Graham**
> (In Bolchover & Brady, *the 90 Minute Manager*, 2002)

FROM GOALS COME ROLES

As we know with teams, they are a collection of individuals. Therefore, for the team to be successful and achieve its goals there is a requirement for all players to make their specific contribution. It is ultimately the player's responsibility to make sure that they have asked all necessary questions of the coaches to allow them to go into a game with a crystal clear picture of what is expected, and perhaps more importantly, what is not expected. The following **Roles Rules** (illustrated in the diagram) will be of help in making sure that communication of roles is always thoroughly covered.

Role Rule 1: Clarity

The first, essential step with roles is to make sure that each player is absolutely clear about what is expected of them. It is possible that lack of clarity can lead to a decrease in confidence and conviction on the pitch, so the importance of getting this obvious step in place cannot be overstated. We've seen the

> Don't assume that everyone on a team shares a common view of what the important team goals are – it is essential that a team keeps open communication channels relating to what the team is about and what it is striving to achieve.

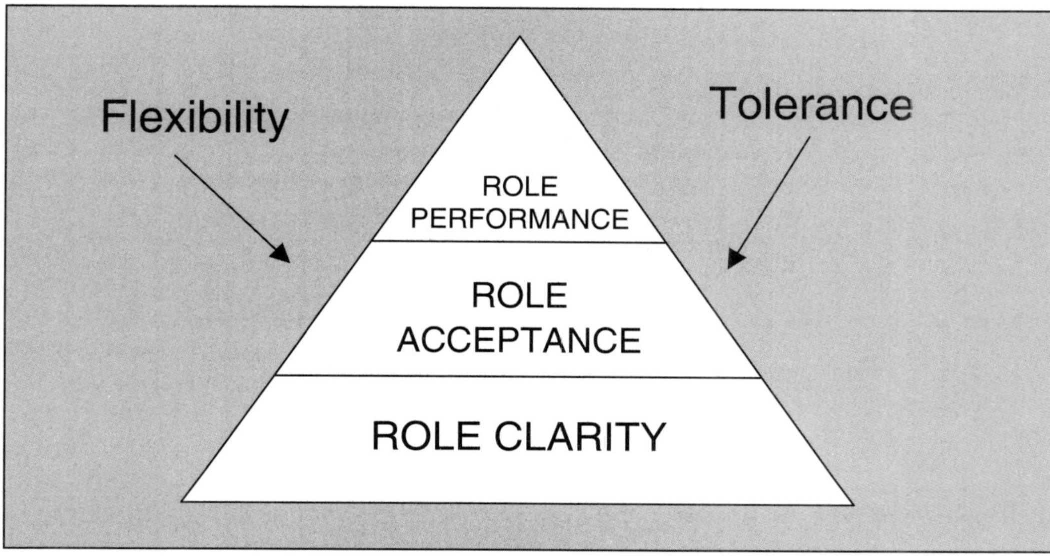

difference that role clarity can make in football, with players with whom we've worked being transformed by changing teams and as a result moving from a situation of lack of clarity and underperformance to a team where role clarity was crystal clear, indecision was removed, and performances were improved beyond recognition. Players have to ensure that they get a full and clear outline of what is expected of them when they are attacking, defending, and at set-pieces. Players also need to be clear in their minds what they should *not* do in their role, or what is *not* expected of them. We often find players have more problems second-guessing themselves because they think they might get berated by the coach for trying something different. The indecision resulting from not fully discussing the role slowly erodes natural, free-flowing play, and is frustrating to witness as the situation can be so easily resolved.

Many players are confused by a coaching instruction to simply 'play your natural game'. It is often assumed that the player in question is aware of what this means and how it will contribute to the team effort – often they do not know but are reluctant to ask for more detail

The situation is perhaps made more obvious by considering a player who plays the same position but in different formations for club side and then representative side. It is vital that in either situation they are totally clear what is expected of them by the different coaches, so that they can move from team to team and still produce a high level of performance. We know players who have moved up a level in standard of play and as a result have assumed something different and special is expected of them straightaway. They have not communicated effectively enough to find out what is actually expected, and have caused themselves to lose confidence as they don't think they're matching up to the new expectations!

Role Rule 2: Acceptance

Once a player knows clearly what is expected of them, the next step is obviously to make sure that they accept the role that they are

Personal Role Checker

Am I totally clear what is expected of me?

In defence: ______________________________

In attack: ______________________________

At our set-pieces: ______________________________

In training: ______________________________

In contributing to the team in other ways: ______________________________

Which, if any, am I not sure I can fulfil? ______________________________

What can I do to increase my acceptance of my roles? ______________________________

Am I clear what is *not* expected of me?(Things I shouldn't do in my role on the pitch) ______________________________

playing, and are satisfied that they have the requisite abilities and temperament to fulfil the role. Players who feel that they are being played out of position, or that their natural game is being compromised through the tactical approach that the team is taking are low in role acceptance and extra work needs to be carried out to ensure that the player realizes how important their role is to the overall success of the team. Hopefully, if it is made clear how individual roles are aligned with the successful achievement of team goals, the players will readily appreciate why they need to fulfil a specific role. Equally, if the player is committed to the shared goals, they will also be able to add a perception of value to their role, even if it is perhaps not the one they would ideally have chosen if they were abe to build the team around themselves.

Failure to check on role acceptance can disrupt team unity, so it's important that we don't assume that just because someone is clear in their goal they automatically accept it. As a player you should be prepared to seek help to ensure that you are both satisfied with the role you have, and understand why a coach believes you have the ability to carry out the role if you cannot immediately see yourself

> In today's football, with 60 matches per year, you really need two complete teams. So the regular players also have to sit on the bench now and then. Some hang their heads, while others go on the stack and want to show what they're really made of when they get the chance to play again. It's important to encourage players in this situation, and talk to them more than usual
>
> **Sven-Goran Eriksson**

doing all that is asked of you. The confidence that someone else has in you needs to be given the opportunity to be passed on, so don't worry about asking questions such as 'What elements of my game do you see that give you the belief that I can play this role in this team?' Coaches need to be prepared to make their decision-making clear to players when they assign roles, so don't be afraid of taking the time to talk through with the players in detail their specific roles and why you believe they are the ideal player for the job at the present time. Communication with players on the bench is also critical as the Eriksson quote illustrates.

Role Rule 3: Performance

If you are clear about your role and accept it and your ability to carry it out, then you can actually get on with performing it. The important element, though, of role performance is how well you, as a player perceive you are carrying it out. Obviously, if you perceive that you're not doing your job well, then you'll lose confidence in your ability to carry out the role, so role acceptance will decrease. Equally, the opposite is true if you perceive that you are performing very well. Although your own perceptions of how well you're meeting the demands of the role are important, you should make sure that you seek feedback from the coaches regularly, focusing on what they think you are doing well, and what they think can be

> This is a team game and I have only achieved what I have because of the people around me.
>
> **Andy Cole**
>
> (*The Times*, 18/5/99)

improved. In this way, you ensure that your own perceptions do not become the only reference point you use. External observers can always provide a useful perspective that you don't always get to appreciate when caught up in the moment-to-moment changes of the match. You'll also appreciate why the personal performance review systems that appear in Step 7 can be so important, because they give you the chance to critique your role performance more objectively. Failure to review regularly and effectively can lead to players losing sight of how well they are performing their role.

Within the team context an element of perceived role importance that needs mentioning is that of appreciating the roles of team-mates. It is not unusual for players to be unaware of the specific demands of other roles in the team and hence be quick to criticize when errors are made. Teams that have a full appreciation of the various demands of different positions usually demonstrate higher levels of cohesion and work better together under pressure. Therefore, there is great merit in making sure that players appreciate and experience what other players have to do in their role. Getting players to play in unfamiliar positions in training is obviously a great idea, a concept that has been so successfully used at Ajax in Holland, where by the time young players have progressed through the ranks of the junior teams they have had experience of playing in all positions on the pitch. Although these players have their preferred positions, they become better all round players by playing 'out of position', and also become better team players because they appreciate

> Gary's a team player. The perfect team player.
>
> **David Beckham** speaking about Gary Neville – what do you think it is that makes Neville such a great team player?
> (*David Beckham: My Side*, 2003)

the critical importance of every position on the pitch.

We also find that it's useful to get the team talking to each other about the demands of individual roles and make sure that players are accountable for helping each other become a more successful player on the team. The Role Commitment and Performance exercise really gets this communication process started, and out in the open. The exercise is also particularly useful because it forces players to get used to talking positively about themselves to their team-mates. The players also make a public commitment to their areas of development, and the rest of the team can hold everyone accountable for the changes they say they need to make. Finally, players publicly recognize that they need the support of team-mates to help achieve their goals. Within this exercise, there is no reason why coaches and other support staff should not be included. You'll also find the exercise very useful in helping to build the various levels of confidence that we introduced in Step 2 that are essential to effective team performance.

> I study their games to see what they can do and what they can't do. I try and help them with what they're not good at, tell them my weaknesses and hopefully we learn from each other. The sooner the partnership clicks the better you're both going to play.
>
> **Teddy Sheringham**, discussing forging a good partnership with another striker

Role Rule 4: Flexibility

Players must also be ready and willing to be flexible in their role performance. There will be occasions when it is necessary for them to play a different role from usual. Circumstances may dictate that they must assume a role tha they do not enjoy and find very difficult. Great teams have individuals who are very aware of when these situations come along and have a team climate whereby everyone is prepared to 'muck in' and do things that may not normally be within their area of responsibility. This is relevant to the training ground, off the pitch and even during matches sometimes.

Role Rule 5: Tolerance

Sometimes one player will need to 'interfere' with another in order to execute a role effectively. Successful teams contain players who demonstrate a high level of 'tolerance' in relation to this interference. In simple terms, there may be a situation where one player needs to sacrifice some training time in order to assist a team-mate. Members of great teams acknowledge that these sort of sacrifices are part of being a good team player and realize that next week a situation may arise whereby the favour must be returned.

Think about how you would rate your team against these five 'roles rules' using the Roles Rules chart.

Exercises such as this and the Role Commitment and Performance exercise create and develop a strong sense of 'team confidence', mutual trust and respect. You will recall the three confidence circles we introduced in Step 2. They are also very relevant in this Step as you can imagine.

How do we score on the 5 ROLES RULES?

1. **CLARITY:** we all are very clear about what is expected of us as individuals.
   SCORE out of 10____________
2. **ACCEPTANCE:** we all accept our role and are confident we can carry it out.
   SCORE out of 10____________
3. **PERFORMANCE:** we are all performing our role effectively.
   SCORE out of 10____________
4. **FLEXIBILITY:** we're good at doing other roles when the need arises.
   SCORE out of 10____________
5. **TOLERANCE:** we are tolerant of interference from others and happy to sacrifice our own practice when others need extra help.
   SCORE out of 10_____________

Role Commitment and Performance Exercise

Ahead of the meeting have all players prepare their responses to the following statements:

1. The three key personal qualities that I bring to the team in my position/role are:
   a.
   b.
   c.
2. The three key personal qualities that I am working on over the next month that will improve my performance in my position/role are:
   a.
   b.
   c.
3. The three key things I need the rest of the team to do for me to help me make these improvements as effectively as possible are:
   a.
   b.
   c.

In the meeting have each player provide their responses to statement 1 in turn. Have someone keep a record of each player's contribution. Repeat the round the table process with statement 2 and 3.

The responses are then transferred onto sheets of paper for each player with every player's statements shown under the headings of:

The strengths that we can expect to be shown week in week out by the players around us are: . . . All players' names and their three statements

The areas that we can expect the players around us to improve on over the next month are: . . . All players' names and their three statements for 2.

As a team we can help each other by making sure we: . . . three statements for number 3 followed by each players' name.

Communication about roles within a team is crucial in developing cohesion. © EMPICS

BUILDING TEAM COHESION

Finding the glue that binds a team together is critical in team success. The shared vision and shared commitment to achieving a goal that we have already talked about is a crucial element of team cohesion – as are the role rules we have just covered. The final piece of the team jigsaw that we must now examine is how the two different types of team cohesion fit together. These two cohesion types are referred to as SOCIAL and TASK.

Social Cohesion is very much focused on how well the players get on away from per-

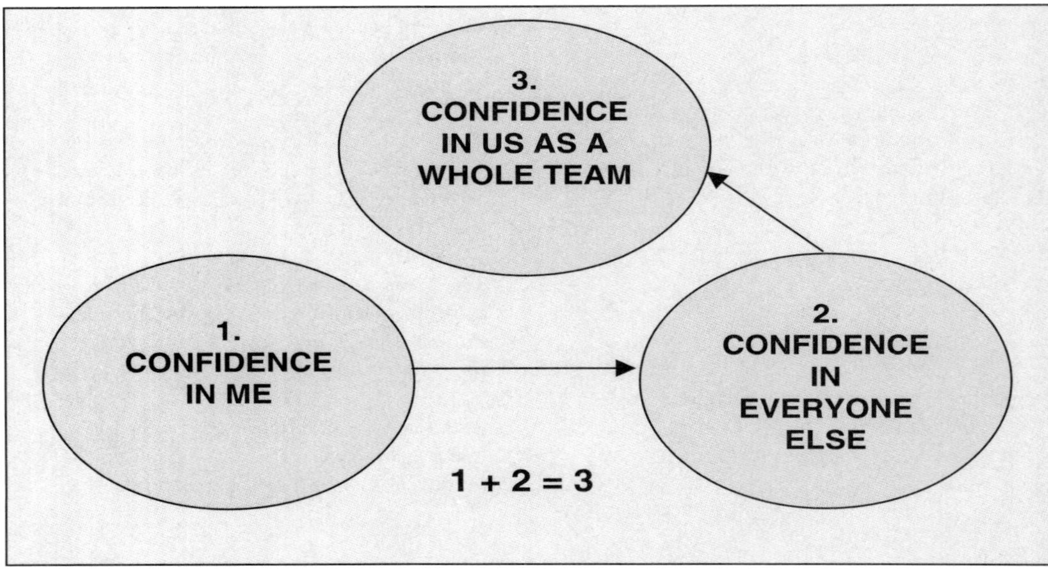

> Human nature dictates that if you have 16 players, two coaches and a manager, they won't all like each other. But that doesn't matter as a long as you can rely on each other. The only way you can do that is by having a great team spirit, so that when you go on to the pitch you have a bond and unity that holds you together.
>
> **Alan Hansen**
> (In Bolchover & Brady, *The 90 Minute Manager*, 2002)

formance and the training environment. From a coaching perspective, it's a lot more enjoyable environment to manage if your players all get on well. However, it's not essential that a team is the best of friends in order to be successful. Perhaps another, less discussed, element of social cohesion is the idea that players might support each other in reaching certain goals. Much like the final element of the role commitment exercise, it is clear that a team within which players support each other in the pursuit of individual goals is going to have a greater sense of togetherness and desire to succeed for each other. Truly cohesive teams recognize that by helping each other, players are helping themselves increase the likelihood of personal and shared success. This support cohesion can be a very important safety net for team spirit.

Alan Hansen's quote at the top of this section sums up **Task Cohesion**. We have never seen a successful team that just got on well and was full of social cohesion. Task cohesion is all about how effectively a team coordinates its efforts to achieve the shared common goal we have stressed as being so important. So, on the one hand we have the shared goal, and the team high in task cohesion is excellent at coordinating its efforts to achieve that goal. Some teams may have the shared goal, but might be ineffective in their efforts to coordinate the available talent. Successful teams always have a high degree of task cohesion. Successful teams don't always score highly on the social cohesion stakes. It's a nice added extra, but not essential. We're sure you know successful teams where the players didn't get on with each other, but on

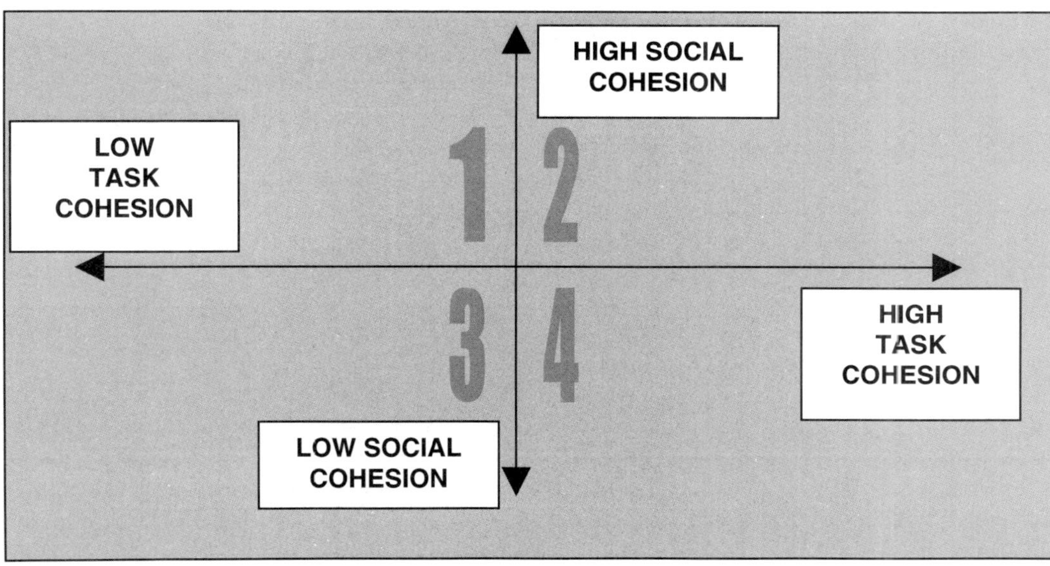

> When Task Cohesion is high, the team has collective agreement and confidence on the vision, goals, tactics, strategy, game plans and individual roles. Players communicate well on the pitch and work together as a cohesive unit.

the pitch they were very close knit in their pursuit of winning.

How do you rate your team on these two elements of cohesion? You can plot your team on the graph. Simply find the point on the line that you think equates to your level of Task Cohesion and then go up or down from that point to the level that shows your amount of Social Cohesion and then place a mark on the graph. You can then answer the question – 'If we are to become a team with a better winning mentality, where do we need to move to on the graph?' Quadrant 2 is where you should be aiming but with an awareness that it is better to be in Quadrant 4 than Quadrant 1.

So, we would not necessarily advise against spending time and money on a paint-balling or go-karting team-building weekend, unless it is at the expense of the important time and effort that needs to be devoted to developing task cohesion.

REVIEWING PROGRESS AS A TEAM

You'll realize by now that the majority of this section actually focuses upon getting teams communicating in order to develop and maintain team spirit. In order to get your team really working well together, encourage teams to use the post-match period to help put some important building blocks in place. Having set the team goals and turned these into match-specific targets, in order to make sure that individual, mutual and collective confidence grows you have to spend the time teasing out the key lessons from performance. Collective learning is critical to team development. Teams need to make sure they have built in time so that lessons are learned as quickly as possible. These are the most successful teams in sport: they don't learn by chance – they make systematic use of experiences, and don't believe that a match is over until they have actually reviewed it and learned from it.

If you set you aims and objectives for a match really well, you will be able to carry out an effective review using the Match Review Agenda that we've presented opposite. The questions are directed towards helping the team learn the main lessons that revolve around:

1. How good they are at actually putting into action game-plans. If a team improves its ability to translate process goals into reality, then its confidence will grow markedly.
2. Recognizing recurring strengths that the team is displaying, that should become an accepted part of the challenge they pose to opponents.
3. Identifying unique learning points from the match that can be built upon in future games.
4. Using the match to help shape positive action for training and preparation in the lead-up to the next performance.
5. Making sure that the team is focused upon processes rather than outcomes in order to help build a more resilient collective belief.

If you want to use a shorter review approach, we would recommend the traffic light review system. This simply gets the team to consider what key things it needs to *stop* doing, *start* doing, or *continue* doing? You can easily apply these questions to the pre-match period, first half, second half and post-match period to provide a more detailed review of the key time periods of the match. If you apply this tighter structure you will find it easier to review the match rather than simply have a free-for-all of

Match Review Agenda. The 10-point Review Plan.

1. What were our key goals for the game today?
    - a. Tactical
    - b. Physical
    - c. Attitude
    - d. Teamwork
2. How well did we achieve our tactical goals? (i.e., can we do what we say we're going to do tactically?)
3. How well did we achieve our physical goals? (i.e., can we put our fitness into action and make it work for us in the way that we say we're going to?)
4. How well did we achieve our attitude goals? (i.e., can we play with the mentality that we say we're going to play with regardless of how the match is going?)
5. How well did we achieve our teamwork goals? (i.e., to what extent did we really support each other?)
6. What did we learn about us as a team from this match that we didn't know before we played it?
7. What did we show again about us as a team in this match that we have already proved is a strength of ours?
8. What did we show again in this match that we still need to be working on in order to become an improved team?
9. Is there anything else that we need to note about how we played, what we did, or what happened that we should learn from?
10. What does our key theme need to be for training over the next week to make sure we stay focused on maintaining strengths and avoiding weaknesses?

opinion being offered for anything that players think is relevant.

With either review approach you can obviously build in your use of video replays of the game, examination of statistics and the opinions of coaches to help inform the responses

Based upon our performance, what key things do we need to STOP doing immediately?

Based upon our performance, what key things do we need to START doing immediately?

Based upon our performance, what key things do we need to CONTINUE doing?

STOP...

START...

CONTINUE...

of the players. Keep in mind that with the reviewing you go through, you are working towards the situation where you can become confident that the team is never going to make the same mistake twice, and they are becoming more aware of how to play to their strengths and get a greater sense of control over producing performances.

As well as reviewing specific matches, you will need to make sure that as you go through the season you review progress towards your goals that were set, and make sure that amendments are made as necessary. All goals should be adaptable to account for varying rates of progress, so you should be open to monitoring progress and adjusting targets to keep motivation as high as possible.

And Finally . . .

In summary, teams generally perform best when they manage to create an environment in which all players feel valued, challenged and supported. Players must understand their role, buy into the team ethic and feel they have the support of their team-mates and coaches. When these things are in place, a team can experience *synergy* – when the whole is greater than the sum of the parts. Don't forget, the best eleven players don't always make the best team. But with eleven great players AND a great team culture, then you have something special!

STEP 7

Match Preparation: When Saturday Comes

> Everyone has a will to win, but very few have a will to prepare.
> **Vince Lombardi** – American Football Coach
>
> Winning can be defined as the science of being totally prepared. **George Allen** – US Sports Writer

Obviously the reason for all the training, the building of confidence, the development of skills (mental and physical) and the time and effort expended in this process is all actually about the 90 minutes of action. From the very first quote in the book, through to this point, we have stressed the importance of preparation, and professionalism. However, you can have a great week of training and preparation, but for some reason on match day itself, something goes wrong, something doesn't feel quite right, and you end up not doing yourself justice on the pitch. This can be hugely frustrating for all concerned. This last step will focus you on the essential sporting quality of on-the-day preparation. Being able to develop a consistent mindset on the day of a match, whoever the opposition might be, is the key to consistent performances. The mantra that you have to start to make use of, and completely believe in is:

Consistent preparation brings consistent performances.

And of course, you know by now that this is going to mean consistent thinking as well as consistent behaviour. Too often we have spoken with players who immediately look to the 90 minutes of the game to try to explain why they played the way they did. Did they get the run of the ball? Was the player they marked having an off-day? Did my lucky socks work for me again? Did the pace of the game suit me? All these kinds of reasons point to the match, or something else, controlling the way someone played, rather than the player controlling the way they play. So principle number one is all about 'taking control'.

There is an old saying that 'familiarity breed contempt'. In relation to pre-match preparation, we believe *'familiarity breeds control'*. Control is the main commodity to possess in the build-up to a match, and you'll see how it can be used to great advantage to bring a solid foundation of consistency to match days.

The challenge for this chapter is to be able to develop a pre-match routine that is in your control and 'portable'. Therefore, wherever you play, whatever the conditions, whoever the opposition, you will be able to control your performance by controlling your preparation. Your match-day routine needs to be seen as a piece of equipment that is as vital as

> If you're successful, 50 per cent, if not more, comes from what happens off the pitch. You need good players but if you've got the same good players as the next coach it's the preparation and the focus that are more important. And this is something Arsene has been very strong on.
>
> **Glen Hoddle**
> describing Arsene Wenger

your boots – your boots travel with you everywhere you go, and for all they know it could be another training session that they are involved in rather than an FA Cup final. A good routine will allow you to be as confident as your boots that you will be able to produce a great performance, regardless of context.

> 'There is a set routine Eriksson goes through on big-match days that begins with a team talk in the squad hotel. 'I talk for about 10 minutes, with lots of repetition. Simple messages about attack and defence, the strengths of the opposition,' he explained. 'Then at the stadium, when you have more than an hour to wait in the dressing room before kick off, it is a time for small jokes and smiles.'
>
> 'I try to talk to each player then, in turn. Last-minute advice, but brief. No more than a minute or two with each one, sometimes only 30 seconds. As the kick-off approaches the players start to clench their fists and encourage each other, which is natural. I don't say anything then, but I try to have a quick last word as the team is going out.'
>
> And what does Eriksson say at that time? What will be his last message before England's World Cup commences? 'Don't be afraid. It is just a game of football.'
>
> **Paul Wilson**
> (*The Observer*, 2/6/02)

GET IN CONTROL, STAY IN CONTROL

When developing a pre-match preparation routine, it is important to make a decision about exactly when the match starts for you. From now on, your matches will begin when you choose that they begin – not when the ref's whistle blows at kick-off. So, your match might begin when you wake up in the morning, when you arrive at the ground, when you sit down in your place in the changing rooms, whenever you choose to start taking control over how you are going to play. Once you decide that you are starting your match, your job is to get in control and stay in control for as much of the day as possible. If you get in the habit early on match day of being in control of what you are thinking and how you are feeling, then it becomes easier to keep this theme going once the match begins.

The idea is probably best explained by examining an example routine. This can be seen opposite, and shows that it is possible to impose a structure on match day that includes pre-match and in-match time. The count-down to kick-off fits in with our idea of 'think about what you're going to think about'. The player has decided how they need to control their thoughts, feelings and actions in the lead up to and during the match, so that they can have the best possible chance of getting into their ideal performance mindset. They are not leaving it to chance that they will think the things they need to think – a plan has been laid out, and now the task is to go out and find out how well they can execute the plan. The ability to carry the plan out is as important as the ability to intercept a through ball, or bury a penalty into the back of the net. Do you know how good you are at putting your plans into action? Is this a skill that you need to be developing? We'd challenge you to set yourself the task of becoming the best player you know of 'doing what you say you're going to'.

It's useful to note that by deciding that your

Countdown to Kick-off – Controlling my Performance

TIME	FOCUS ON . . .
13.00	Arrive at ground and go straight to changing room. The match begins here for me. I'm preparing better than the opposition. Unpack kit and look through personal goals for today's match. Visualize first passes, first tackle – conviction and quality theme. I'm in control.
13.30	Get into shorts and socks, begin stretching. Take my energy drink and energy bar. Enjoying the build-up and doing everything at my pace.
14.00	Rest of kit on other than shin-pads. As I put my boots on, reminding myself how well I've prepared this week, focusing on the quality of training and how good my fitness is this season.
14.15	Out onto the pitch. Going through structured warm-up with ball and sprint work. I'm really in the match now – by the time the kick-off comes, I'm going to feel like I've been in the game 10 minutes already. Visualizing best recent performance highlights as I warm up. DO EVERYTHING WITH 100% QUALITY. Start getting into my ideal performance mindset – check and change if needed.
14.40	Back in for the team talk. Positive self-talk all the way now – looking through personal goals again as I listen. Feeling totally in control. Positive and ready.
14.55	Out onto the pitch – last warming up, eyeballing the opposition, seeing myself in the game now, taking them on, playing to my strengths.
15.00	Kick-off – You've been in control for 2 hours already – stay in control, time to put plans into action – keep backing yourself, time to enjoy.
15.50	Half-time. Sit down, relax, energy drink and quick review – positives, negatives and pointers. Keep mind lively and ready to go back into battle.
16.00	Second half. This is your time. Stamina and skill mean you're more of a threat this half. Stay focused on the processes.
16.50	Game over – back in and listen to initial talk. Re-fuelling and stretching while listening. Staying in control – whatever the result.
17.00	Go and do 10-minute warm-down before coming back in to shower.

match starts when you want it to, it is possible to spread the pressure of the 90 minutes out over a much longer period of time. You can put pressure on yourself to get your preparation as effective as possible, and if the build-up is actually part of the performance, you can feel like you are taking positive action and 'performing well' from much earlier in the day.

We know players who like to start taking control the evening before a match by doing some structured visualization, and getting their kit bag packed and everything ready for the next day's travel. The choice is completely individual, but needs to be thought about – what is right for you to make sure you are mentally peaking for the start of the match?

Obviously kick-off is not always at 3.00pm and matches are not always at the same ground, so you need to make sure that any routine you have will work for you at different times and against different opposition. These factors are just part of the inconsistency that we have already talked about and add to the challenge of you seeing how good you can be at being the consistent factor in the inconsistent world of sport.

So, it's worth revisiting your pre-match preparation and making sure you have a very well-thought-through plan of how you'll take control. You control your thoughts, you control your choices, so make some strong decisions about what your ideal match preparation looks and feels like. By getting this element of your game right, you can have a competitive advantage before you even step on the pitch. We'd argue that this is one of the easiest elements of preparation to carry out in a 'professional' manner – you don't have to be a high-earning player to be able to have a professionally structured build-up to a game. There's little point spending all that time training and preparing if you're then going to just 'see what happens' on match day.

> Everyone learns from Eric. He's a great trainer . . . A lot of players who just used to go home after training sessions, have seen how hard Eric works and they do stay out longer now and practise their technique.
>
> **Ryan Giggs** speaking about Eric Cantona
> (In Balchover & Brady, *The 90 Minute Manager*, 2002)

ARE YOU PROFESSIONAL?

Once again . . . not, 'Do you get paid for playing?', but, 'Do you take responsibility for making your performance happen through controlled preparation?'

Examples of Professional Choices

- Having a nutritionally balanced diet that allows the body to work hard in training, to recover properly and peak for matches.
- Arriving at training on time in a frame of mind that is not distracted by events away from training and ready to train with maximum quality.
- Using time the night before a match to think through taking on the opposition, preparing kit and getting high quality rest and sleep.
- Behaving towards team-mates and coaches in a way that expresses confidence in their abilities and in a way that allows them to prepare themselves effectively.
- Taking responsibility for errors in training and matches, and planning how to eradicate them from your future game.

Being professional relates to the choices you make about how you spend your time, how you treat other players, how you eat, sleep and control your thinking. Ultimately, preparation is the responsibility of the player to get it right. Unprofessional players will let other people and outside influences affect the quality of preparation, and will not make choices to promote ideal performance mindset.

You can look at the professional approach to preparation examples that we've provided to help you make judgements whether your pre-match routines are being backed up by professional thinking.

My Commitments to Excellence	Name: Date:
Personal **R**esponsibility **I**n **D**elivering **E**xcellence	
What I need to remember. What I need to focus on in order to get the most out of myself in the game. How I need to make sure I am playing as well as I train.	
Fitness and physical preparation Insert statements that identify fitness strengths and recent positives about fitness levels.	
Technical and tactical preparation Insert statements that identify skill and tactical strengths.	
Mental readiness and mental fitness Insert statements that identify key thoughts to remember and key mental strengths/attitudes that will underpin performance.	
What I'm in control of that will make a difference What I need to stay focused on – controlling the controllables.	
How I will contribute to the team Specific targets for the match – personal goals.	
My Commitment Statement Insert personal motivational reminder.	

My Commitments to Excellence	Name: *Jim Striker* Date: *21/07/2004*

Personal **R**esponsibility **I**n **D**elivering **E**xcellence

Remember to control the game . . . don't let the game control you.

Stay focused on the next pass, the next shot, the next tackle . . . stay in the moment!

Review training – know my strengths and plan how to put the strengths into action.

Fitness and physical preparation

Great speed over 5–10 yards. Upper body strength is best ever – I will not get knocked off the ball. I know I have the stamina to play for 120, never mind just 90!

Technical and tactical preparation

First touch and snap shots on the turn – catch the defence cold.

I've studied the defence, I know where their weaknesses are.

Stay strong in the air, and always pushing onto their last man.

Mental readiness and mental fitness

Never give in . . . 100% commitment throughout.

I know I play well when i stay calm and focused . . . make sure I control my temper with the stop technique.

What I'm in control of that will make a difference

I trust my pre-match routine – I control everything about it and I will get it spot-on at the weekend. Control the preparation = control my performance.

How I will contribute to the team

Shots on target will be over 65 per cent.

I will keep talking throughout – never let the encouragement die.

I can bring the other dangerous players in around me by keeping pushed onto the last man.

My Commitment Statement

I will set the professional standards for the team on and off the pitch.

MATCH PREPARATION PLANNERS

Some players also find that a more general 'match commitment' planner can be very helpful for them to take control over their pre-match and in-match mindset. We have used these simple summary sheets in a variety of sports, and they help performers to capture the key thoughts that need to be driving their performance for a match or a series of matches. The charts can be filled in by the player independently, or one to one with a coach. They are simply designed to help the player stay focused on the critical thoughts for them when Saturday comes. We've attached a couple of sample charts that you can easily

Performance essentials	Name: *Dave Keeper* Date: *23/11/2004*

Personal **R**esponsibility **I**n **D**elivering **E**xcellence

Key personal challenges to take on

Positive on crosses — seek them out, don't hide from them.

Improve speed of distribution when ball is in my possession.

What people watching will see in my game today

Physical: *Strength and power in all areas of my game — speed of reactions too.*

Tactical: *Directing the back four with conviction, creating attacks from defence with quick ball.*

Attitude: *Dominant presence in the box — commanding and always positive, whatever!*

Strengths that always show through – my signature strengths

Shot stopping and big presence in the area.

Communication with everyone around me.

Self-talk reminders for pre-match

Training prepares you for this. The quality of work there has more than prepared you — keep the belief and lead from the goal.

Personal Commitment Statement

Whatever the score, there will be no difference in my body language or self-belief. My ability determines my belief, not the score in the match.

adapt, but you'll notice that they act as a summary for the player, getting a lot of information down to the basics, and very much focused on the player taking control and making strong choices about *how* they are going to play.

The planners simply pull together a variety of information that can be shared between player and coach to make sure that thought processes are kept simple in the lead up to the game, and only the essential details are being focused upon. After a week of training and a lot of information being passed on to players, it's important to make sure that the information has been boiled down to the essential performance thoughts. Having a clear, focused mind on match day is very important, and these simple summary planners can help players develop focused thinking.

Another theme of the planners is that of focusing on strengths on match day. As we've alluded to in the book already, it's important that players are not going onto the pitch with the intention of making sure that their weaknesses are not exploited. The planners make sure that you are focused on strengths – what is good, what is working well, what will allow you to play well, and how you'll put these strengths into action. This complements the 'in control' mindset we've already talked about as you are 'choosing' the way you *are* going to play, rather than making sure that you are *not* going to make certain errors. So, as we discussed in Step 2, it's critical that players know their strengths and are used to making sure that these feature in their match thinking.

CUE CARDS

The previous two examples of match-day reminders might be a little lengthy for some players. Another way of focusing on effective pre-match preparation is by using personalized cue cards. These can be of credit-card size which the player can read through quietly during the build-up to the game. The cue card contains simple reminders of the main factors that help the player get in control and stay there for the match. Cue cards can be updated regularly, and once again help the player develop clarity of thinking in a time when the pressure is possibly building. They are a simple idea that is worth taking the time to experiment with. The content of the cards is very personal, but we find that it's good to get a mix between a simple instruction, an attitude statement and some strength reminders. The cards tend to work well when they have room for match-specific reminders to be written on them. Once you have the card, they're easy to update and are easy to read through as many times as you need before a match and during half-time.

FUNDAMENTALS IN THE PRE-MATCH PERIOD

We'd recommend that you develop your own approach to mentally warming up for a match. However, here are some elements that we think are worth considering for inclusion in your build-up. These things will make sure you are not 'hoping for a good day', but are checking the key details that will help you make sure you are taking the professional option of controlling your controllables in the lead up to the match.

1. Wake up with a positive state of mind
Get in the right frame of mind from the moment you wake up. Work out how to start the day off by thinking positively. 'Training's over . . . it's time for action. Let's make the preparation worth it.' Choose a statement that works for you and start the day confident, positive and looking forward to the challenge.

2. Kit Check
Make sure you have everything packed that you are going to need. Avoid last-minute

Example Cue Cards

YOU WILL SUCCEED BECAUSE . . .

- You work harder than anyone you know.
- You are at your fittest ever.
- You never give up.
- First touch, vision and control are your strengths.

Match Specific Reminders

-
-
-

PLAY WITH P R I D E

ALWAYS . . .

- Strong first tackle.
- Beckham-like work-rate.
- Test the opponent . . . don't be tested.
- More time than you think . . . clear head, relax.

Match Specific Reminders

-
-
-
-

Passion + Process = Success

SUCCESS

- **P**roduce under pressure – use the pressure.
- **O**pportunities are there to be taken.
- **W**ill power for the full 90 minutes.
- **E**xcellence is a choice.
- **R**elentless quality – never say die.

Stay focused on your game, your qualities.
The team needs you at the top of your game.

frantic searches for essential items. Maybe make a list that lives in your kit bag so that you can check everything off as you put it into the bag. You might even begin to associate bits of kit with positive images from past performances, so when you pack them in the bag, your mind recalls the personal highlight.

3. Baseline emotion check

At some point in your routine, make sure you take a bit of time to check how you're feeling. Are you psyched up enough? Excited enough? Worried enough? You may make these checks several times, but you have to make sure that the checks are timed right so that you get the chance to make any changes to your emotional state. Don't leave the check too late so you can't make the alterations you need.

4. Confidence Check
Use your list of positive affirmations, or cue cards to keep your confidence level stable in the build-up to the game. Choose your thoughts, and back yourself.

5. Mental Rehearsal
We've already mentioned you might want to visualize as you pack your kit bag, but it's well worth deciding when you visualize and what you visualize. This is a great opportunity to lay down the blueprint of how you're going to play today. 'You get what you see', so make sure that you programme your mind at some point in the lead-up to the match.

6. Meals
Everyone knows the importance of the pre-match meal, so make sure you get advice on what is nutritionally ideal for fuelling you up, and when you need to get food and drink into your system. You might want to think about other fuel going in prior to the game and during half-time. Get advice from fully qualified sports dietitians, and use your meal as an important confidence-building block.

> Back (a key member of England's victorious Rugby World Cup side) is obsessive about it. Everything is about training more effectively and then recovering better in order to train effectively the next day. 'Until recently, we would still have a couple of pints after a match and the next day we wouldn't think about nutrition,' he said. 'The next day now we're thinking we've got to get at least 6,000 to 7,000 calories in us so we can train most effectively on Monday.'
>
> **Owen Slot**

> I always prepare myself with an Elvis song and I try to bring a little bit of his magic on to the pitch. He is my eternal hero and I dedicate all my goals to him.
>
> **Ole Gunnar Solskjaer**
> (*The Daily Telegraph*, 9/9/02)

7. Physical Warm-Up
Make sure you create a sense of familiarity through your physical warm-ups. Wherever you are, you will be able to carry out the same physical routine, and this is the time when you are 100 per cent sure of feeling that you are doing the things that consistently get you feeling physically and mentally right for the kick-off.

8. Allow for individual differences.
It's difficult in team sports to let everyone do exactly the preparation that they want to. However, players need to take control of the pre-match period and work out how they are going to individualise the team preparation. You have to make sure you get personal benefit out of the collective build-up and players need to respect that there will be differences in the changing room. So don't judge other people for doing slightly different things . . . only judge them if they never do the same preparation from week to week! Then you know they're not going to perform consistently!

'WHAT-IF?' PLANNING

Although we recommend developing robust pre-match routines, things often don't run smoothly in the lead-up to games. Whether it's a delay in traffic on the way to the match, a broken bootlace, or a floodlight failure, routines can be disrupted. The fact that there are going to be disruptions is predictable, so

Consistent preparation is the key to achieving success on match day.
© EMPICS

Example 'what-if?' scenarios

What if . . .

- A bootlace breaks as you are tightening them up ready to go out ten minutes before kick-off?
- The team bus breaks down and you arrive at the ground fifteen minutes before kick-off, when you would normally have ninety minutes?
- Your coach unexpectedly shouts at you during the pre-match talk?
- Your team-mate whom you usually rely on to keep you calm with some jokes in the lead-up to the game becomes ill at the last minute and can't play?
- During the warm-up, you just can't seem to stop thinking about a personal problem that is concerning you?
- Immediately prior to the start of a game, someone tells you that a national team selector is here to watch you today?
- There is a floodlight failure five minutes before the start of the match and kick-off is going to be delayed by twenty-five minutes?
- You have an argument with a team-mate on the way to the match about the game you played at this ground last season?
- The hotel you are staying in will not serve your lucky pre-match meal?
- The opposition have made sure your changing room is really cold and uncomfortable before kick-off?
- A player from the opposition threatens you during the warm-up?
- A team-mate gets injured in the warm-up and you have to change position in the final few minutes before kick-off.
- An official is injured and the beginning of the second half is delayed while a replacement is found.

it's important to make sure you plan for how you will deal with any that are thrown into normal preparation time. In fact, if you get really good at dealing with disruptions you can begin to see this as another advantage you have over your opponents. 'We know we can deal with hassles better than the opposition, so bring on the disruptions!'.

You can prepare for how you would deal with disruptions by using 'what-if?' planning. In other words, spend some time considering, and even discussing as a team, how you will cope if you experience a range of disturbances to your normal build-up. You can then make decisions about what you would do when these or similar disturbances occur. The event then becomes a helpful reminder of what to do, rather than something that causes confusion and indecision. If it helps, you could consider how the most cool, calm and collected player you know would react to these kinds of situations.

We've provided some typical 'what-ifs?' that can be considered by individual players or teams. What would you do? How would you react to stay in control . . . remembering that it's not the problem that produces an impact upon performance, but rather your reaction to that problem. Therefore, you need to think, 'How do I need to react?', 'How can I use this event to be a positive rather than a negative?'. In some instances, you may already have solutions to the problems, and if this is the case, this should let you know that you have some good habits in place already.

As a team you can use 'what-if?' planning to help with considering how you are going to counter different team formations, and how you might deal with performance situations (that is, having a player sent off fifteen minutes into the match, or going 3-0 up after twenty minutes). Don't just think of negative scenarios. You can prepare for things going a lot better than anticipated. The more you individually and collectively prepare for different eventualities, the more you will build your confidence so that you can respond to any events with a cool, collected mind, and so that your 'what-if?' ability is excellent, regardless of the context.

> Boss Kevin Keegan is unwavering in his desire to reach that stage and so despatched former England captain Stuart Pearce to Poland on a spying mission.
>
> 'Stuart has been over there to look at the training pitch, the stadium, the travelling times, the hotel, and what we can find near to where we stay to use on the morning of the match,' declared Keegan.
>
> 'We want to go as far as we can in the UEFA Cup and we must not leave anything to chance.
>
> From: www.Manchesteronline.co.uk

WHAT IF? Scenario 1

As captain of your club side your own form is suffering despite the team doing very well. You are starting to feel guilty about not contributing and your confidence is becoming shaky. You cannot figure out why your form has deserted you and are desperate to overcome your slump. What do you do?

WHAT IF? Scenario 2

You are captain of a team that is on a losing streak. The team has experienced bad luck as well as playing poorly. Your two most senior players are out of form. You overhear a conversation between a small group of players in which your captaincy is being questioned. What do you do?

The 'what-if?' planning lets you know that any routine you do develop for match day has to have flexibility built into it, so you need to know what the essential things are that you need to focus on in your build-up in case you don't get to carry out the full count-down to kick-off as normal.

If you like, you can use the 'what-if?' planning idea for wider performance issues. Consider these two scenarios, and work out what your plan of action would be.

You can learn a lot from these kind of scenarios, so we'd recommend using the idea for the wider development of your winning mind, as well as helping you to prepare for match day.

Two Big What-ifs?

Getting Put on the Bench When You Weren't Expecting It

This happens to most players at some point so you must be prepared for it. We won't dwell on the issue here but simply provide you with five top tips for dealing with this frustrating situation.

1. Recognize the contribution that you can still make and ensure that you are absolutely clear regarding what your role is and what it might be should you get on the field.
2. Stay confident by focusing on your reminder statements and using positive self-talk at all times.
3. Identify exactly what you can control and work hard on doing the best possible job on these things – for example, contribution to team meeting, quality warm-up, support for other players.
4. Keep talking to your coach and manager – don't hide away. Let them know that you are still 100 per cent committed to the team goals.
5. Be ready to play at any time. Warm-up well and make sure you're mentally ready to switch on at a moment's notice.

Getting Injured

When you initially get injured you're likely to experience a series of strong emotions such as denial, anger and frustration. These will pass and you'll then be able to focus on coming to terms with the injury and how you are going to cope with the rehabilitation period – whether it be a few days, a few weeks or a few months. Again, we won't dwell on the issue here but if you want to read more, we devote a whole chapter to the subject in one of our other books – *The Mental Game Plan: Getting Psyched for Sport*, the details of which are at the end of this book. What we will say here, though, is that when you are injured it is an ideal opportunity to do lots of visualization practice. Here are three of the most important things you can visualize when you're getting ready to return to full fitness.

1. Playing your first match back and performing really well.
2. The injury healing and your body actually getting stronger.
3. Some aspect of skill development that you may have been neglecting recently.

Doing lots of visualization like this will help you avoid the type of feelings that Michael Owen describes in the quote below.

AFTER IT'S OVER – MATCH REVIEWS

In Step 6 we focused on team reviews. It's just as important to make sure that efforts are

> I had never had an injury until this year and when I got the injury I didn't know what it was about. When I came back the first time I was a nervous wreck. The psychological side is the worst.
>
> **Michael Owen**
> (*The Times*, 24/5/00)

made to learn as much as possible from each performance from an individual perspective. Players who review and learn from their performances become much more aware of issues and areas for development, as well as balanced in their knowledge of what is working well for them. Although the individual review can seem onerous to carry out, it is well worth the time on a number of levels.

1. First, as in Step 1, the review fits in with the process of goal-setting, that is, Set–Do–Review. So, it's an essential part of the professional approach to developing a winning mind.
2. The reviews become a very important record of performances that can be used in preparation for future matches. For example, when you review a match against specific opposition you are documenting valuable knowledge that you can draw upon next time you play them, whether it's a home or away match. Without recording the information, it is less easy to recall the key pieces of information in the build-up to the next game against them.
3. Reviews serve to help with 'parking' the match in the past. If reviews are not carried out, and action plans laid out, it is possible that errors or concerns arising from the performance keep coming back because specific action has not been decided upon in relation to combating the problem.
4. Reviews ensure that players systematically build their knowledge of what makes them tick and how they produce a performance. The process makes players realize that they are responsible for their performance and maintains the sense of control and momentum so essential when striving for ongoing development as a player.

Personal Match Reviewer

Date:__________ Venue:__________________ Kick-off:________ am/pm
Opposition:__________ Conditions:__________________________
Half-time:_______ Full-time:_______

Personal Performance Level (%):_______ Team Performance Level (%): ________

Period	Negative	Positive	Action
First 25 mins			
Remainder of first half			
First 25 mins of second half			
Remainder of second half			
Overall Performance			

Match Reviewer

Preparation Review *(Remember, how you prepare influences how you play).*

How well was normal routine stuck to?

What differences occurred?

Did these differences make a difference? Positive? Negative?

After Preparation/Warm-up, what were you feeling/thinking?

Compared to your best preparation ever, how good was this preparation?

Specific Match Target Review (How well did I do what I said I was going to do?)

Future Match Reminders:

You might now want to carry out the reviews on your own, so feel free to get someone who watches you regularly to help out, or exploit your coach's expert view of you. However, remember, you have to develop your own view of your performance, and use other people's perceptions to provide you with information, rather than *the* answer.

You have to begin to trust your own judgement more than anybody else's – but it's great to decide whom you listen to and whom you don't listen to. Football is a game of opinions, but as a player you have to trust your opinions, and know when other opinions can be disregarded as uninformed nonsense!

The review sheet we've provided is designed to kick you off on your own process of reviewing, and gets you to break the game down into quarters so that you can think through 'How well did I achieve my targets in each phase of the game?'

You can record positives and negatives in terms of achieving the targets, as well as decide what action, if any, needs to be taken. You only need to identify key positives and negatives, and make sure that you decide what you are going to do to amend the negatives and maintain the positives. The Action Points can relate to what you are going to do in training the following week, or what you will do next time you play. Either way, you are identifying positive action, which means you are making strong decisions about how to build from this performance. You might even want to use some of the action points to become part of your next cue card to be used in the next match.

You should keep all of the reviews together in one place so that you can easily look back over a number of matches at once.

We'd recommend that you carry out the review the day after the match, so that you can reflect on the performance as objectively as possible. If you carry out the review too soon after the match is over, you might find your perceptions are skewed by the result, or your own post-match emotions.

The reviews will also help you to start to appreciate where you can make improvements in your winning mind, so you'll be able to make sure that the reviews are helping to point you towards the specific *Steps* in this book that need improvement. If you want to take control of your development as a player, then we think that the review process is essential. The most impressive players we've worked with have a fantastic insight into their own games – self-awareness is a great strength of theirs, and there's no doubt that if you review, self-awareness grows, and as a result your ability to manage yourself improves too.

AFTER THE MATCH . . . DEALING WITH THE MEDIA

To conclude this chapter we shall briefly review the issue of dealing with the media. This is a factor that plays on some players' minds, so we thought it appropriate to

Ten top tips for dealing with the media (although you will benefit from specialist advice for certain live interviews to camera or microphone)

1. View dealing with the media as part of the 'performance' and accept that you need to do some preparation for it. As you know, if you're prepared, you'll perform better, be less nervous and more confident.
2. Ask as far in advance as possible what the media are going to be asking you about, how long it is likely to last. This will give you an idea of how much information to provide in your replies.
3. If possible, ask what the first question will be so that you can have an answer prepared.
4. Memorize up to three things that you want to get into the conversation and make sure you raise them even if they are not directly related to a question – say what you want to say!
5. Slow your speaking down by trying to go at half your usual pace. Everyone has a tendency to speak faster when being interviewed.
6. Don't be afraid to pause before answering a question. Most people dive in and have to think as they speak.
7. If the interview is being pre-recorded, don't be afraid to stop your answer and start again. The media wants you to come across well and will be quite happy to stop the tape and allow you to start over.
8. Make sure you 'finish' a sentence. Many people have a tendency to continue 'waffling' until the interviewer interrupts them. Try to be as succinct as possible. Make your point and then stop.
9. Be confident – back yourself to do a good job. Even do some visualization from time to time to rehearse media 'performances'.
10. Ask the interviewer for some feedback afterwards to help you improve for next time.

> In football virtually everything is on view; what is not on immediate show is soon revealed by almost permanent media attention.
>
> Bolchover and Brady in *The 90 Minute Manager*, 2002

> There is always a headline that judges you, whether you are innocent or guilty. It is very difficult to live like this. Eventually it wears you down.
>
> **Sir Alex Ferguson**
> (In Bolchover & Brady, *The 90 Minute Manager*, 2002)

provide some commonly used advice. As players become more successful, the amount of media interest will increase, so it's important that this doesn't become a hassle, or distraction from performance. Preparing for competition should therefore involve competent handling of the media that should have two clear angles. First, promoting yourself, the team and the sport in a positive way. Second, being able confidently to deal with the media when they approach you so you avoid the feelings described in the quote by Sir Alex Ferguson.

CONCLUSION

So there it is. You've now completed the 7-Step Guide and should be ready to achieve new levels of performance excellence. This won't happen overnight but with regular practice and commitment we're confident that you'll notice a significant difference in how you feel about yourself as a player and how you perform on the football field.

Remember the ABC of mental training to get the most out of your 7-Step Plan:

A pply the various techniques to your own individual needs and challenges

B elieve in yourself and your training at all times

C ommit yourself to fully making your mental skills work a fundamental part of your performance preparation.

Best wishes and enjoy the challenges!

Where To Go Now?

Having gone through the 7-Step Guide, here are a few other books you might enjoy reading:

Beswick, B., *Focused for Soccer* (HKP Europe, ISBN: 0-7360-3002-6).

Bull, S., *Sport Psychology: A Self-Help Guide* (The Crowood Press, ISBN: 1-85223 568 3).

Bull, S., Albinson, J. and Shambrook, C., *The Mental Game Plan: Getting Psyched for Sport* (Sports Dynamics, ISBN: 0-9519543-2-6).

Eriksson, S.-G., Railo, W. and Matson, H., *Sven-Goran Erikkson on Football* (Carlton Books, ISBN: 1-84222-613-4).

Whitaker, D., *The Spirit of Teams* (The Crowood Press, ISBN: 1-86126-051-2).

If you'd like to contact the authors of this book use these websites:

Steve Bull:
steve.bull@lane4.co.uk

Chris Shambrook:
chris@headstartconsulting.co.uk

Acknowledgements

The authors wish to recognize, and acknowledge, the following publications for providing the quotations used throughout this book.

Beckham, D., *David Beckham: My Side.* (CollinsWillow. 2003)

Bolchover, D. and Brady, C., *The 90 Minute Manager: Business Lessons from the Dugout* (Prentice-Hall Business, 2002).

Cantona, E. and Fynn, A., *Cantona on Cantona* (Manchester United Books, 1996).

Dalglish, K., *Dalglish: My Autobiography* (Hodder and Stoughton, 1996).

Eriksson, S.-G., Railo, W. and Matson, H., *Sven-Goran Eriksson on Football* (Carlton Books, 2002).

Ferguson, A., *Alex Ferguson: Managing my life* (Hodder and Stoughton, 1999).

Redgrave, S. and Townsend, N., *A Golden Age* (BBC Worldwide, 2000)

Jonny Wilkinson: The Perfect 10 DVD (Empire Media Productions, 2003).

The Daily Telegraph

The Sunday Telegraph

The Times

The Sunday Times

The Guardian

The Observer

The Independent

The Independent on Sunday

The Daily Mail

Index